Breaking the Code

Stop Looking for Answers and Start Enjoying Life

Rusty Gaillard

To Alex, for your love, patience, and endless support.

Table of Contents

INTRODUCTION 11

CHAPTER 1: FORGET RETIREMENT 13

THE CALL OF FREEDOM... 18

SOMETIMES YOU HAVE TO CRASH 21

HOW WILL YOU RESPOND?.. 27

CHAPTER 2: THE CODE 31

RAISE YOUR LIMIT.. 36

PAY ATTENTION 39

ONCE YOU LEARN YOU CAN NEVER FORGET 42

CHAPTER 3: YOU ARE CREATIVE.................................. 47

THE POWER OF BELIEF.. 52

EMBRACE YOUR CREATIVITY.................................... 61

CHAPTER 4: BREAKING THE CODE 71

DECISION 72

DISCOVER YOUR INNERTECH................................... 76

FOLLOW THE C.O.D.E... 79

DEBUGGING... 121

SIMPLE, NOT EASY 124

CHAPTER 5: SHOULD I STAY OR SHOULD I GO? 127

CHAPTER 6: IF NOT THIS, THEN WHAT?...................139

CHAPTER 7: AM I LIVING SOMEONE ELSE'S LIFE?....151

CHAPTER 8: AM I WORKING TOO HARD?..................163

CHAPTER 9: IS IT TIME FOR A CHANGE?...................175

CHAPTER 10: NOW WHAT?...187

YOU HAVE EVERYTHING YOU NEED 196

ABOUT THE AUTHOR 199

ACKNOWLEDGEMENTS 201

ONE LAST THING... 203

Introduction

I wrote this book for my fellow A-students. For you who have worked hard your whole life to check all the boxes. You went to the right school, earned a practical degree, got a respectable job, and climbed the ladder. After so many years of hard work, after so much progress, when you should have "arrived", you still feel like something is missing.

You did everything you were supposed to do. You followed the path that your parents, siblings, friends, and mentors laid out for you. But you find yourself wondering what's next. Is this all there is? Why am I working so hard?

If life doesn't have the same spark it used to, this book is for you.

Having been in that place, I learned that life can continue to have spark, passion, and purpose. To find it, you have to ask different questions. When you give yourself permission to explore possibilities and

11

ideas that you had previously thought were off-limits, you may find the path to fulfillment and passion right in front of you.

There is nothing wrong with you for feeling stuck, trapped, on a treadmill, running hard and not going anywhere. Most successful people reach this point. The only question is what you do when you get there.

You are doing exactly the right thing by picking up this book. My hope for you is that when you put it down, you will have a direction that rekindles the flame of passion, commitment, and purpose in your work and your life. That flame never went out. It's just waiting for you to rediscover it.

Chapter 1: Forget Retirement

I remember the day I told my boss I was leaving Apple after 13 years to become a transformational coach. It was Friday and I told myself I would talk to him before the end of the week. I was nervous. As much as I was excited about my new direction, this was still a risky move.

He must have had a full schedule that day because I wasn't able to connect with my boss until late in the afternoon. I finally tracked him down in his office. I took a deep breath, sat down, and cut to the chase. I told him I was leaving to do more personally meaningful work. Then I waited for his response.

I was pleasantly surprised to find him supportive and interested. He asked about my goals and shared some of his own projects to make a difference in the world. It was a positive interaction, and I felt encouraged.

As I started sharing my plans with others more broadly, about 10% of my colleagues had a similar reaction to my boss. They were inspired by my decision to walk away from it all. I was leaving a steady paycheck as a respected leader at a great company where I had worked hard for my success. I was at the top of my MBA class at Stanford. I put in the work and was a Worldwide Director of Finance, responsible for the sales forecast for all Apple products globally.

By all external measures I had arrived. Yet I was leaving.

Many people would love to have the kind of success I had, yet I was going in search of something better. These people respected and admired both my vision and my courage.

I understood them because I felt the same way about the people who had gone before me. Watching a young finance professional leave a promising career at Apple to work for the NFL. Watching a tenured analytical expert leave to study and practice holistic and herbal medicine. I had been that person who looked on with awe and a tinge of jealousy as these people left successful and promising corporate careers to "follow their passion". Could I make a change like that? What would I do?

As it was my turn to branch out on my own, I heard echoes of those same questions in the conversations I had with others. They wanted to know how I reached this decision to leave, how I found my next path, whether I was nervous about it. As I looked into their eyes I could see the gears turning, wondering what a similar transition might look like for them.

Another 10% of my peers were clearly intimidated by my departure. There were no gears turning in their heads, only closed doors. They didn't ask me how I reached this decision, they challenged me. Was I sure I was doing the right thing? Did I worry about walking away from a paycheck and benefits? Was my family supportive? They saw only risk and they shied away from it. Rocking the boat felt threatening, and they didn't even want to be near someone who was making waves for fear of getting wet. Some of them even avoided the conversation. We focused on the content of our work together right to the last day. It was safer for them.

The remaining 80%, the vast majority, were neither inspired nor intimidated. They simply looked at me like I was from another planet. They were curious, but they didn't want to get too close. They couldn't imagine doing what I was doing, it was so foreign to them and their approach to life.

Perhaps you have watched someone make a career transition like the one I made. Or perhaps this is the first time you're hearing a first-hand account of a change in direction. Either way, it's important to notice your reaction.

Stop for a minute right now and ask yourself:

> If you were my co-worker at Apple, which group would you be in?

Are you inspired by stories of people reinventing their lives, are you intimidated by them, or is it so foreign you can't relate?

When you hear of someone changing direction, do you wonder for a moment if you could do the same, or do you rule that out—believing it's ok for someone else, but not for you?

How you answer those questions is a reflection of how you view the world—what is possible, reasonable, or sensible. **This is your code**. It's been programed into you through years of experience and instruction, and it controls not only your perception of the world but also how you respond to events and circumstances. Think of your code like an operating system on a computer. It can provide new expanded functionality, but it can also limit the full use of the hardware's capability. Most importantly, it can be upgraded.

The Call of Freedom

In my last few years at Apple, I would think regularly about the R word: retirement. I day-dreamed about what I would do. I could manage my own schedule, pursue my interests, finally have time to do the things I wanted in life. Not that I had a long list of activities I wanted to pursue—I was too busy to think about that. I just knew that I longed to be in full control of my life.

Retirement was pretty far out, so I also thought about other jobs I'd like. Maybe if I left my job at Apple I could find another position that alleviated the stress and anxiety of working at a big company.

Mailman kept coming to mind. I'm good at getting things done, so I thought I could get through my route pretty quickly and efficiently. There would be no laptop to take home, no email after work, nothing to worry about on vacation. The idea of a job that I could do without much effort and turn off completely after hours appealed to me.

Of course I knew there were parts of being a mailman that I wouldn't like... but the low expectations sounded great. All I had to do was show up and finish my route, with no further expectations of me. Gone would be the drive for more, continuous improvement, climbing the corporate ladder.

It took me years to realize that being a mailman was really about freedom. I wanted to feel free to follow my heart, to enjoy a slower pace of life, to do what felt good instead of rushing to check off the endless to-do list. A slow pace and following my heart were not part of my daily life, and I wanted more of them.

I didn't have the nerve to seriously pursue becoming a mailman, so I kept coming back to retirement.[i] It would be the ultimate freedom. I could do exactly what I wanted to do, and I didn't have to worry about work or the commitments to anyone else. I remember asking my dad, when he was well into his retirement, if he didn't want to do something more impactful with his time. He was such a smart and capable man, he could have made a big mark on the world. His response surprised me at the time. He said, "I spent 40 years working for someone else, with very little time for myself. This is my time." He was talking about freedom.

Very few people feel free to choose how they spend their time. They have so many obligations between work and family that their personal interests don't get fulfilled. Work now, enjoy life later. With that mentality, retirement is an important topic of conversation for most people.

Just like your reaction to me leaving a safe and steady job at Apple, how you think about work and retirement is a reflection of your beliefs about life. Pause, take a breath, and consider how you think about the arc of your career.

> Do you believe in the delayed-gratification approach to life, where you sacrifice now for reward later in retirement?

Do you believe you have to wait for retirement to experience freedom and fulfillment?

Do you believe you could have a job where you are happy, free, and no longer focus on retirement as the end goal?

Once again, your answers to these questions are a reflection of your code.

Sometimes You Have to Crash

I searched for years looking for the job that would be engaging, challenging, meaningful, and provide the freedom I wanted. I looked at other big tech companies, startups, consulting, even considered being an independent finance consultant—but none of these really scratched the itch I was feeling. Until I found the path to become a coach.

Tears came to my eyes when I received my coaching certificate in 2018. I stood there in the darkened ballroom, supported by a group of experienced coaches circling the outside of the room, each holding a small glowing light symbolizing the light we bring to the world through our work. I walked back to my spot after crossing the stage, and I looked down at my name on the certificate.

A hundred glowing lights illuminating the room, gentle music playing, my certificate in my hands… and my eyes welled up. I savored the moment, but I was also curious. Why was I so emotional? I graduated at the top of my class from both Princeton and Stanford, both more rigorous and challenging academic experiences, but I didn't feel emotional when I got my diplomas. What was different this time?

As I stood there, tears in my eyes, the answer came to me. <u>Becoming a coach was 100% my choice</u>. Until that point in my life, I had followed a path of success that my family, friends, and teachers valued and supported. It was so engrained in my code for success that I never truly chose it. I simply executed it.

It's easy to make a choice that meets with others' expectations. When I left my first job to get an MBA at Stanford, the people around me understood it implicitly, just as they did when I joined Apple. But to leave a great job to start my own business? It made no sense.

It is not a rational career move to leave a successful, high-paying leadership job at a great company to start your own business. It is not common to leave a job as an expert to start again at the bottom. But in the two years since I left Apple, I have not thought once about retirement. I found work that is meaningful, challenging, and allows me to live the life I want *today*, without waiting for the freedom of retirement.

> *You don't see possibilities that you don't believe are possible. They are invisible to you.*

I had to step outside of my corporate perspective to see coaching as an opportunity. Until that point, it

<u>wasn't even in the possibility set.</u> The jobs I considered were corporate jobs, consulting, perhaps working at a startup. I had never even considered being a coach because it was not compatible with my code. It was effectively invisible to me.

That may sound extreme to you, but it's how your code works. You don't even see possibilities that you don't believe are possible for you. Ideas that go against your code are rejected subconsciously, without a true conscious evaluation of them. They are invisible. That's what happened to me.

I thought hard. I brainstormed. I talked to other people. I tried to figure it out. But the only ideas I had were similar to jobs I had done in the past or had seen my peers do. I could take incremental steps in a new direction, like working at a startup instead of a big corporation, but other paths were hidden from me.

I had some help changing my view of the world when my wife decided to get divorced. I had worked incredibly hard to make our marriage work:

24

individual and couples therapy, even a therapy center in the woods in Kentucky, trying to figure out how to be a better husband and save our marriage. It didn't work.

I used the same approach trying to save my marriage that I used in all other challenges in my life: hard work, determination, persistence. Yet I failed. The code for success that had carried me so far in life crashed. Not only that, the rosy picture I had of my successful life fell apart. My ideal life with a good job, a happy marriage, kids, nice vacations—it all came crashing down around me.

I was embarrassed. I felt like a failure that I couldn't keep my marriage together. I had looked down on people who got divorced as being weak—that they didn't have the strength or commitment to stick it out. Yet there I was, getting divorced despite bringing all the strength and commitment I had. I had done everything I knew to do, and I had failed. Unequivocally.

My divorce was incredibly painful and challenging for me. It challenged my self-image, broke apart the life I wanted to lead, and caused me to question how I had lived. The rules of success I had followed didn't seem to work anymore.

It hurts to confront failure and difficulty in life, but sometimes you need a crash to wake up. A crash can be a sudden event, like getting divorced or being passed over for promotion. But it can also be a slow gradual building of dissatisfaction: weakening or eroding relationships, giving up hobbies, feeling bored at work, even mild depression. While this can be painful, it's also good news. It's an invitation to upgrade.

You don't have to wait for things to get bad to choose a life of fulfillment and purpose. You can upgrade by choice because there's something you *want* from life. Trust me—the path of pain, difficulty, and struggle is exactly that: painful and difficult. Don't wait to get pushed into a change because life gets hard. Choose to step forward towards a life that calls you, towards something you really want. Towards freedom.

How Will You Respond?

Your code serves you, and it holds you back. It allows you to see some possibilities, and it prevents you from seeing others. It determines whether you believe your career is all hard work and sacrifice, waiting for retirement, or whether you could love your work. And it controls your reaction to others as they embark in a new direction.

If you want to achieve a new level of success, you have to **break the code**. You have everything you need to break through your old way of seeing the world and welcome a new level of success and fulfillment. The only question is: will you?

When confronted with a new opportunity, your old way of thinking creates all sorts of reasons why not to go forward. Trust me—I've heard them. Will I lose everything I worked so hard to get? I can't start again from scratch. Am I putting my family at risk? What if I fail? As you confront your code and step outside it you are sure to hear these, or similar, thoughts.

How you respond when you hear those thoughts will determine your trajectory. Will you listen to those concerns and decide to stick with the status quo? You know where that path leads. It's a well-known path of certainty, but it's missing the magic you may be searching for. Or will you decide to break through the barrier of your old way of thinking and give yourself permission to explore a whole new level of success? The success is yours for the taking. The only question is whether you're willing to grab it.

If you're ready for a change in your life—to feel more clarity, engagement, and passion for your life—the rest of this book will give you the process for achieving it. It's as simple as breaking and rewriting the code. The first section, chapters 2 through 4, will explain what the code is, and how to break it and rewrite it. The second section, chapters 5 through 9, has examples of people who have gone through this process, with some additional tools and suggestions you can use. The final chapter, chapter 10, addresses what comes next after the book.

As you read, don't just consume information. Apply it in your life. Let your imagination go to work, step outside the constraints of your current way of thinking and living, and imagine a whole new level of success beyond what you've experienced to date.

Life is precious, and you deserve more than biding your time until retirement. You have everything you need to create a life of freedom that aligns with your values and serves your greater purpose in the world. And you can do it with confidence. Let's get started.

Chapter 2: The Code

We all have a code that we live by. This is not something abstract or esoteric. This is biological. From an early age you learn how the world works. You watch your parents, your family, the people around you, and they demonstrate to you how things work. You learn how to resolve conflict. You learn how to display affection. You learn how a couple gets along. You learn about work—whether you work at home or from an office, whether you wear a suit or jeans and a t-shirt. You learn about money—how easily money comes, whether money is an important factor in life, how you talk about it. These learnings become your perception about life, your understanding of the "code" of life which governs how the world works.

Technology is also built on code, the rules that govern how a software program works. But in artificial intelligence (AI) and machine learning, the code also has to be trained. For example, if you want to teach an AI algorithm how to recognize a cat, you train it on millions of images. The algorithm guesses whether it's a cat, and you tell it if it's right or not. Soon, the AI begins to recognize what is a cat. Your brain has been trained in fundamentally the same way, through seeing patterns of life, over and over again, over decades. You have come to learn what is possible in life.

Let's take a simple example. If I were to ask you how easy would it be for you to double or triple your salary, what would you answer? Most people would say they don't think it's possible. Why is that? Because they don't know how to earn multiples of what they make today. Let's say you currently earn $100,000. If you knew how to earn $300,000 you would be doing that already. But you're not. The problem is not a lack of opportunity. There are plenty of jobs that pay $300,000. The challenge is that you do not yet know what it takes to get one of those jobs.

Making a significant improvement in your life requires change in two dimensions. One dimension is the *external results*—the changes in your life that you can observe, like going from $100,000 to $300,000 in salary. But to achieve that upgrade in your external results, you first have to upgrade *internally*. If you see yourself as $100,000 a year kind of person, you will never earn $300,000 a year. All changes in your external results start with internal upgrades.

To use an example from my own job search, I spent five years looking for a new job in finance and supply chain. Yet every job I found, even offers I received, felt like more of the same. They were a change in scenery, but not what I truly wanted to do. Why is that? I saw myself as a business person, primarily someone who worked in large corporations. Other kinds of jobs, like being a coach, a teacher, or a chef, were not even in the realm of possibilities. It's not that I considered them and rejected them—they never occurred to me as possibilities. That was my

33

code at work. It was my belief about who I am and the kind of work I do.

All the results in your life come from
your code.

All the results that you have in your life—your health, your relationship, your work, your career, your free time—come from your code, what you think is possible. If you have any doubts about this, look around you. Certainly there are people in your life who have what you want: the freedom, the career, the close relationship, the physical health. It is possible. You know that because you see it in the world around you. So why isn't it possible for you? I'm sure you have all sorts of reasons why you don't have everything you want in life. You can list the many things that stand in your way: not having the time, the money, the connections, and the experience.

The problem isn't with the challenges in your life. The problem is with your belief about the challenges.

The real answer why you don't have what you want is that your code isn't compatible with the things you want. The problem isn't with the challenges in your life. The problem is with your belief about the challenges. If you believe they will hold you back, they will. Just like if you believe you will never earn $300,000. To achieve a new level of results in your life—in any aspect of life—you must adopt a new belief.

Breaking the code is the first step to achieve a new level of success in your life, but you don't live without a code. That would be like never learning to ride a bike and having to think about each step every time you got on the bike. It is not a practical way of living. After breaking the code, you get to rewrite it—in a more empowering and expansive way. You get to upgrade.

Raise Your Limit

If you are wanting more from life, that is your invitation to upgrade. You break and upgrade your code because your current results aren't satisfying anymore. Whether you have a precipitous crash, or you recognize things are heading in the wrong direction and choose to make a change, breaking and upgrading your code starts with a dissatisfaction with the results you have in your life today. It starts with desire.

Desire for a different result is what drove every invention across time. Think about the light bulb, the car, the computer chip, the cell phone, plane travel, space travel. These inventions were created out of a desire for improvement in some area of life: communication, transportation, and lighting. Once a person (or a small group of people) became focused on solving that problem, they found a new path forward that had previously not been seen.

Technically, every "invention" has been possible for thousands of years. There is no law of physics or law of nature that was created or modified to enable any of these things to come into existence. The fundamental laws of aerodynamics that govern airplanes have existed for all of time. The Wright brothers did not create new laws of nature. They simply discovered new ways to harness and interact with the laws of nature that have always existed.

Every invention requires only a person or group of people who have the belief, and who are committed enough to embrace an idea and take the steps necessary to bring it to fruition. From that perspective, you can argue that these things were never invented at all. The capacity for them always existed. The true invention was not the creation of the thing itself, but rather the knowledge, the way of thinking, and the way of working with the materials and physical laws of the universe that enabled them to come into being.

In other words, when we say a new gadget was invented, what we really mean is that a new manner of thinking was invented. The new thinking enables the manipulation of materials and laws of nature into a new form, which we see as a gadget. The introduction of the iPhone in 2007 was revolutionary, yet the raw materials, electrical engineering principles, and logical principles that underlie the iPhone have existed for thousands of years. The invention was in how they were put together and used to create what we call the iPhone. The invention was a way of thinking, a process.

What does that mean in your life? It means that everything you want in your life is possible today. The raw materials, the laws of nature all exist for you to have exactly what you want. There is no external constraint. <u>Everything you need to achieve a new level of success in life is available to you right now</u>. The only thing that needs to change is for you to have a different way of thinking and operating with the world around you. You need to raise the limit on what you think is possible.

Your code is the only thing standing between you and an even more rich and rewarding life. Just as with any other invention ever created, everything required to achieve a new level of engagement and satisfaction in your life is already available. Go back to the example of the $300,000 job. Those jobs exist today. The only change required is to transform yourself from a $100,000 person to a $300,000 person. You have to upgrade your awareness and your thinking. You have to upgrade your code.

Pay Attention

If this upgrade process were easy, you would have done it already. As a smart and curious person, you would have already achieved everything you want in your life. Even with so many good things in your life, you still are searching for a deeper sense of meaning and fulfillment. Life can look great from the outside, but a piece still seems to be missing.

It can be tempting to ignore those subtle feelings that something is missing, or to talk yourself out of them. You have had such great success in your career so far. You're paid well, work at a great company, have a good network of friends, have a promising future... these are convincing reasons to feel grateful for your life. You may think something is wrong if you still feel a sense of longing for something more meaningful or deeper.

You are not wrong for wanting more meaning, purpose, and alignment in your life. If you're feeling those pulls for more, pay attention. That pull for growth and expansion in life is perfectly natural. The cycle of life is one of expansion and growth through the peak of your life, when shrinking, decay, and ultimately death arrive at the end of the cycle. There is no homeostasis. You don't coast or rest. Either you are growing or you are shrinking.

If you feel a pull forward, even if it's a small quiet voice inside you, pay attention. Listen to it. That is your voice of inner wisdom speaking to you, calling you to the next level of fulfillment. If you ignore it, push it away, convince yourself that you already have a good life and it's not prudent to disrupt your comfortable lifestyle, you are squelching your spark of life.

The small voice for more, calling you forward to a bigger and fuller expression of your true self in the world, is precious. Listen to it, honor it, and cultivate it.

Every invention, every novelty, every new experience starts with desire. You have to desire a fuller, richer, more expansive life experience or you will never overcome the inertia of your current habits and beliefs.

You live by design or you live by default.

If you never break the code, you will default to the same patterns of life that have guided you this far in life. You will blink and another five years will have passed. Next year will look much like last year, and the decades will go by in a blur.

Living by design means embracing your innate ability to grow, expand, and develop an even more rewarding life. It means taking 100% responsibility for your life, making your own decisions. It means tuning into your heart's desire. If you want a life of freedom, purpose, meaning, and deep fulfillment, you must start with desire.

Once You Learn You Can Never Forget

As a child, desire drove all kinds of growth and learning. Think of your experience learning to ride a bike. You must have had a strong desire to learn to ride a bike, or you would not have tolerated the multiple failures along the way. Desire is the fuel that enables you to break and rewrite the code.

The first time you got on a bike you fell. You did not know how to ride it. You had to think about it, you had to learn it. But now, if you've ever ridden a bike, it has become second nature to you. Your body knows how to do it without thinking. You don't have to concentrate on your balance and how you pedal and steer. You don't have to consciously think about the interaction of your legs and your hands and your head as you pedal down the street. You simply get on, point towards your destination, and go.

That very same approach is true for you and the $100,000 job today. You know how to get it. You don't have to think about the pieces and how they interact to reach the destination. You simply point in that direction and go. You know how to do the steps and you do them automatically.

The challenge for you is that you do not yet know how to do that for a $300,000 job. Most people want to know the formula, the steps they can follow. Just like riding a bike, there is no formula. A list of things to do isn't going to help you learn to ride a bike any more than it will help you get a $300,000 job. It's not the steps that are the magical ingredient. The secret is the willingness to see yourself as a $300,000 person.

There's no one set of steps, no single recipe. Just as there is no single recipe for creating a microchip, a cell phone, or a car. There are many different ways to create them in the real world. In the same way, there are many different ways for you to bring about a $300,000 job in a way that is appropriate and suitable to you.

What stands between you and a whole new level of success is your code. If you want to achieve a new level of success, you have to rewrite it.

There is no limitation to what you can create. Any idea that you have, any dream that you have, any goal is possible, no matter how big or small you consider it to be. Most of my clients can easily imagine another person living in their ideal life, but it's hard for them to imagine it for themselves. If it's possible for anyone, it's possible for everyone. The only obstacle is the code.

You are not short of resources or opportunities. The possibilities are all there. Right now, today, what is missing is inside of you. It's awareness, confidence and belief, and the knowledge that these things are yours for the taking. When you achieve that awareness and knowledge, you see yourself as a new person operating at a different level. Just like you would upgrade the operating system in your phone or your computer to enable all manners of new functionality and capability, you can do the same thing with yourself as you increase your awareness, your confidence, and your belief in possibility. You can operate at a whole new level of success.

Chapter 3: You Are Creative

I skipped kindergarten because I already knew how to read. I have an older brother, and we watched Sesame Street together on TV. I am naturally competitive, so whenever they showed words or letters on TV, I tried to say them before my brother did. You could say I learned to read by competing with my brother at Sesame Street.

I skipped over kindergarten and started right in first grade. I was put in the gifted and talented program where I was pulled out of the classroom for special opportunities for the small group of us who were identified as gifted. I guess it wasn't enough, since a few years later my parents pulled me out to put me in a private school on the other side of town.

From the earliest years of my life, I was recognized for my intelligence. Of course I wanted to develop it as much as I could. It's what made me special.

In high school and college, I prided myself on being the first to turn in an exam. It wasn't just about getting the best grade I could, it was about doing it faster than anyone else. I focused on being faster, smarter, more clever, and more insightful than others. I saw education as competition—not necessarily to learn, but to win. I defined myself by my intellectual accomplishments, as an A-student.

Long before I built the self-image of a high-achieving A-student, as a baby I would lie in the crib and sing when I woke up. That was not an expression of intelligence. That was all heart and body. Joy, life, creativity flowing out of me. My dad would look at me, happily singing there without any worries, and assume I wasn't smart enough to do anything more than manual labor when I grew up. He used to say, "You'll be the happiest ditch digger in the state."

I grew up with that same belief: that joy and intelligence don't go together. That belief was a primary reason I worked through lunch for most of my career. As much as I enjoyed my co-workers, I believed there was a trade-off to be made. My co-workers could either see me as intelligent *or* as fun and happy. My choice was clear.

My drive, focus, and intelligence carried me far, all the way to Worldwide Director of Finance at Apple. I was quick on my feet. I recognized patterns, I often had the best answer faster than others. I still saw myself as the A-student. I was proud of being smart, and I believed that was the path to my success.

It took a trip to the woods in Kentucky for me to confront the limits of my intelligence. I had tried to think my way through life, including my marriage, and I failed. My marriage ended and I reached a dead-end in my job that I couldn't think my way out of. I reached the limit of what I could accomplish just with my intellect. Persistence, hard work, cleverness—the code of an A-student—failed me.

You may not have reached the same end point that I did, but you may be able to relate to the thoughts of

49

an A-student: excelling academically, intellectually, striving to be among the smartest in the room. That may have come easily to you, or you may have worked hard at it, but I'm sure you attribute your success in life largely to your ability to think through a problem and arrive quickly at an insightful answer: to being an A-student. And it has worked.

The problem with this approach is that you are leveraging only a part of your full ability. Your heart and your body are what guide you to a meaningful and fulfilling life. You can't reason your way there. Just like when you order in a restaurant, you don't order from your rational logical brain. You can't reason your way to whether you want chicken or fish. You may try to convince yourself that the fish is healthier, but you know what you *want*. You have to apply the same approach when considering the life you want.

Your heart is your emotional center, and it will guide you to what you like and don't like. Your emotions are your friends. Listen to your disappointment, frustration, and anger. They tell you what you don't like. Your joy, laughter, and happiness point you toward what you enjoy and would like to increase in your life. Emotions are a reaction to life. When you have an experience, or even remember or imagine an experience, pay attention to your emotions.

Your body is the seat of your intuition, which helps you set the direction for your life. It's your gut that pulls you towards the fish or the chicken. But how closely do you listen to your gut when it comes to what you want in your life? Most people will try to rationalize their way through a career plan. You can't reason your way to a career any more than you can reason your way to a satisfying meal off the menu. You have to listen to your gut.

Think of your intellect, your emotions, and your gut as dials you can adjust. Just like adjusting the bass, treble, and mid-range settings on a stereo, there is no single "right" mix. You have to experiment to find the mix that works best for you. If you're a successful ambitious business person, you most likely have been way over-indexed towards intellect. Turn up the volume on your emotions and your gut.

The Power of Belief

Look at the below statements and note whether you agree or not.

- I always have enough money to do what I want
- Family is more important than career, promotions, money, or external success
- Being a janitor is as good a job as being a marketing director
- It's safer to work for a big company than to start your own business
- Work hard and sacrifice now, and you'll be free to do what you want in retirement
- Do work you love and you'll never work a day in your life

You have a quick, almost instinctive reaction to those statements. You know instantly whether you agree or not, without much thought. That's because they all touch on your beliefs about life. Yet you almost certainly acknowledge that another person may have a different set of beliefs and react to the prompts above differently. Those people with another set of beliefs are not wrong. They simply have a different view on the world.

Your beliefs are the foundation of the code that determines how you respond to the world. The important fact is that there is no right and wrong to your beliefs, and they're malleable. They are something you can change.

In the early 1900s a group of people formed a movement called the Transcendentalists. Their fundamental belief is that you have something inside of you that is capable of transcending the conditions in the environment that you're in.

This is a trait that is endowed to all people. We have the ability to mold and shape our environment in a way other animals do not. A bird can build a nest, perhaps use a stick as a tool to access food, but that is the extent of its ability to shape the environment. Even a monkey, our nearest biological relative, has a very limited ability to mold and shape its environment. But as a person you have unlimited capability to do that. You can transcend whatever environment you are in.

This is important to realize because where you put your belief matters. If you believe something is impossible, it will become impossible for you. There are three simple reasons for this.

1. You don't try. You will never even try something that you believe is impossible. If you believe that a $300,000 job is out of your reach you will not even apply.

2. You undermine yourself. If you do apply, you will undermine yourself. Approaching a new activity with doubt, skepticism and hesitation means you will not bring your fullest and best self. When you bring less than your fullest and best self to an endeavor that is new or unfamiliar to you, your likelihood of success goes way down.

3. I told you so. The moment you have any stumble or failure, it reinforces your belief that this was not meant for you in the first place and causes you even more hesitation and doubt.

Your beliefs determine how you approach a new challenge. If you act half-heartedly, with hesitance and caution, you are likely to get half-hearted results, which only reinforces your beliefs.

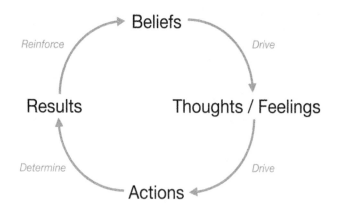

FIGURE 1: THE BELIEF CYCLE

If you know how to ride a bike, you step onto the bike with confidence because you believe you will be successful. When you are, it reinforces your belief that you know how to ride a bike. Consider another example. Assume you don't know how to swim. If you jump in the water with hesitancy and fear, you're only going to bring a portion of your potential as a swimmer. You may struggle and fail, which will reinforce your belief that you were never meant to be a swimmer in the first place.

Your beliefs determine the level of success and the kind of results that you create in your life, which reinforce your beliefs. Your beliefs become a cap on your experience in life.

Open your mind to the belief that there is a creative capability in you that is greater than you ever imagined. Not creativity in the artistic sense, but creativity in the sense of your ability to create a quality of life that you want.

You can understand the creative potential of any person by looking at innovators. Thomas Edison, Gordon Moore, Steve Jobs, Jeff Bezos—these people all created innovations and companies that defied common beliefs. They had an idea, and they had a belief that it was possible. They believed that they could transcend whatever limitations were standard thinking of the day.

This is not a common way of thinking, but it's a powerful way of thinking. Many clients come to me constrained by their way of thinking, believing that their environment or situation is what holds them back. Progress and freedom come from recognizing their inherent ability to shape their life.

When I met Susie, she was living in Silicon Valley working at a biotech company, and she was unhappy. What she really wanted was to build a home in Panama. She had a family connection there, and she had always dreamt of living there near the beach. She knew what she wanted, but she couldn't see any path from her biotech job in Silicon Valley to a home in Panama.

That's a common way to think—focusing on how hard it would be to have what you really want in life, how long it would take, or how much sacrifice is involved. As long as you believe it's hard, the belief cycle guarantees that you will find that it *is* hard. Believe that you can transcend any challenges and create the life that you want. As a creative being, you can design your life without constraint.

The number one ingredient that you need to be successful in creating the life you would love is: break the code of what you think is possible. Start with the belief that you are creative, and you can create an amazing life, even if you don't know *how* to do it today.

Most people find it easier to imagine another person achieving their vision than to imagine themselves achieving it. That is actually a good sign. It means that you know it's possible, since you can imagine another person with that level of success. Perhaps you even know someone in real life. If it's possible for another person, it's possible for you. You have to shift your belief to one of possibility and potential, but you can do it.

As for Susie, she believed that she could create the life she wanted, with a home in Panama. Not long after we started working together, the pandemic hit. She was one of the people who found some benefit in it; working remotely meant that she could also work from Panama. Step by step, she secured the property, met the neighbors, established herself, and hired an architect to design her home. When she shifted her belief from "wouldn't that be nice" to "I'm doing it", she realized her goal.

There are no right and wrong beliefs. You are entirely welcome to believe that you cannot have a $300,000 a year job or a home in Panama. I will not argue to convince you to believe otherwise. But I will point out that by holding that belief, you are making it true. There's no right and wrong here. There's only cause and effect. You can choose to hold whatever beliefs you wish. Recognize, however, that there is an effect of holding those beliefs. You choose empowering beliefs or limiting beliefs. You choose to believe that there are things that are out of your reach, or you choose to believe that anything is possible. Your beliefs matter, and you get to decide what beliefs to embrace.

It takes no more energy to believe that you are creative than to believe you are limited. Why not believe in your inherent ability to create and live an abundant life?

Embrace Your Creativity

Your inherent creativity—the ability to direct your life energy to create a meaningful life—is deeper and stronger than you might imagine. When you tap into it, you will find that the world often responds in a favorable way, supporting you in reaching your goals.

I've attended church for much of my life, and after my divorce I was looking for a new spiritual community. Despite having attended church for many years, I have a healthy dose of skepticism about being told what to believe. I was looking for something new—a spiritual community where I could connect with my sense of a greater meaning in life, but without the rules or dogma. So I went church shopping.

I intended to visit each place once, then decide after visiting 10-15 churches. The fourth place I visited was Unity Palo Alto. I liked it enough that I paused my church shopping and decided to keep going back. It was just a few weeks later that I heard a talk that changed the direction of my life. In a simple 20-minute speech I found a new direction. Within a year I had left my 25-year corporate career to become a full-time coach.

The talk was by Felicia Searcy, a guest speaker at Unity. Her talk was about creating your Ultimate Life Now. She challenged me to think outside the box about my ultimate life, and to challenge my normal reasons for why I couldn't have it "now". It was so meaningful that I can still picture myself sitting there. I can see the blue color of the benches, the other people around me, Felicia on the stage. I remember the feeling of opening my eyes after the meditation exercise with an energy and excitement for my life that I hadn't felt in years.

I never expected my church or spiritual community to change my life in that way. I had never heard of Felicia Searcy before, and I could not have planned or anticipated that our lives would intersect that Sunday. Yet that intersection changed the direction of my life.

> *You can't connect the dots looking forward. You can only connect them looking backwards. So you have to trust that the dots will somehow connect in your future. You have to trust in something, your gut, destiny, life, karma, whatever, because believing that the dots will connect down the road will give you the confidence to follow your heart, even when it leads you off the well-worn path, and that will make all the difference.*
>
> *— Steve Jobs*

Looking back, I can connect the dots. I see that my divorce led me to change churches, and my curiosity about exploring new types of spirituality led me to Unity. Something about the energy there attracted me, and despite attending a traditional church for much of my life, I followed my heart and decided to stay there for a few weeks. My decision to keep coming back meant I was there when Felicia Searcy was there, to hear the speech that changed the direction of my life.

I created this result in my life, but I didn't do it alone. I listened to my desire for a change, I was willing to explore something new, and I followed my heart by changing plans and ending my church shopping spree when I found a place that resonated with me. But I was not responsible for Felicia Searcy being there that day. That part of my story was created by someone else.

When you step forward to create something new in your life, when you embrace your inherent creativity, live from it, and take action, you will be met by the creativity of the world around you. Circumstances, meetings, and coincidences occur to support you. You create your own luck.

Your personal creativity is connected to the creativity of the world around you. Said another way, there is something bigger than you at work in this world. If you don't already recognize this, ponder for a moment the miracle of life that you experience daily. Your body, comprised of trillions of cells, works seamlessly to sustain your life. Your stomach, lungs, heart, kidneys... every part of your body works automatically, without your thought or attention, creating life. The common factor among all of these trillions of cells is your life energy: unquantifiable, but essential.

Your life energy is not something you experience most of the time, but it is what sustains and animates you, giving you the ability to create another day of life. It is that innate creativity of life that causes the trillions of cells in your body to interact and reproduce in exactly the right way to keep you alive and alert. And when that creative energy leaves you, you die and your body returns to dust.

Many people who have been present at a birth or a death describe a spiritual experience of the energy of life entering or leaving this world. You can sense a thinning of the curtain between this physical human world and whatever lies beyond it, as the energy of life enters or exits a human body. It's hard to put into words, but I felt it both at the birth of my son and the death of my father. I felt the magic of life beginning, or ending, right there in front of me. These experiences confirmed a simple truth about our lives as people.

You are blessed with the creative spirit of life. It transcends your human experience, because it is separate from your past, your body, your feelings, and your thoughts. It entered your body at birth and leaves your body at death.

For each of your living days, the creative energy fuels your very existence. It is a power for growth, regeneration, and creation. It is the energy that keeps your body intact, regenerating trillions of cells daily, literally creating you anew every day. Creativity is a life force inside of you, and you can access it to create the kind of life you want to live.

> *The fear of death follows from the fear of life. A man who lives fully is prepared to die at any time. —Mark Twain*

Creativity is the opposite of your code. Your code constrains you with existing habits and patterns; creativity calls you towards new experiences. Your code is based on the past; creativity is forward-looking. Your code is based on what exists; creativity is forming something out of nothing. Your inherent creativity is what enables you to break the code.

The challenge for most people is that they define themselves based on their past experiences. I grew up in Minnesota. I graduated as an aerospace engineer from Princeton. I played soccer growing up. I worked in supply chain and finance for most of my career. I am a father, a friend, a son, a brother, a member of my community, a coach. These are all attributes of my experience. I can be aware of them, but they are not me. You can strip these experiences from me and I will continue to exist. The same is true for you. You are not defined by your experiences or your labels. You are more than that.

You are a creative being. You are blessed with life, and you can harness that energy to create whatever experience you want. You are not limited by what you have or have not accomplished. You are not limited by the labels you use to describe yourself. You are not limited by how much money you have. You can create anything you want.

If you still have a hard time believing this, think of others you know—either personally or indirectly— who are creative. This can be innovators in tech, like Steve Jobs or Elon Musk. They can be social innovators like Martin Luther King, Jr. They can be media figures like Oprah. Or they can be local figures with the neighborhood baseball field named after them. Wherever you look, there are people who have created tremendous things. Those people do not have anything more than you have. You have the same mind and emotions they do. You have everything you need to create an amazing life.

You are meant for more than survival. You are meant to create. No one else has the same vision for creation as you. Explore it. Express it. Live it. Be it.

Chapter 4: Breaking the Code

I was asked recently to divide my life into three equal segments, and to identify the two most positive memories from each segment. Being 48 years old, my three segments were 16-year increments (0-16, 16-32, and 32-48). In doing this exercise I realized that I had many more memories from the last segment of my life than from the first two. There were major life changes in that last segment: getting married, the birth of my son, getting divorced, becoming a Director at Apple, becoming a coach, entering my current & best ever relationship, buying a house. Narrowing it down to just two events in that part of my life was challenging. I had to leave the world of the intellect and go to the heart.

Your heart will guide you to what is most powerful for you. When looking back over past events in your life, certain times or events will stand out. For me, I can picture myself in certain moments, like the moment in Unity when I discovered the path of becoming a coach. I can picture the building, I know where I was sitting, and I can see the speaker at the front. These significant moments of life stand out because they have emotional weight. The moments that touch you, that impact you, that change the direction of your life—you remember those moments.

My hope for you in reading this book is that you experience one of those moments; that you have an awakening of the creativity within you that guides you forward to your next level of success. These kinds of experiences don't happen inside your comfort zone. They require breaking the code. But it is within your reach, and I sincerely hope you find it.

Decision

Nothing happens without decision. It is the first step to any progress in life. Such a simple concept is easy to dismiss but making better decisions can propel you forward in life.

The challenge for many A-students is they tend to over-think decisions. Mary was interviewing for a new job, but she liked her current job. She had worked there for several years, she liked the company and the work, and she felt loyal to the team. She was facing a decision—whether to move forward with the interview—and she felt stuck. She was intrigued by exploring something new, but she felt guilty about leaving a company and a team that she liked. She couldn't reason her way to a decision because there were valid arguments on both sides.

One of the simple but powerful tools I recommend when facing a decision is to imagine yourself 20 years in the future, looking back at this moment in time. Ask that future version of yourself what decision is best for you. Your future self usually knows very quickly.

Learning to trust your heart and gut is not easy for most A-students. They want a decision framework—something they can analyze and come to a rational decision. They want to be able to defend their decision with logic.

The problem with decision frameworks is they are easy to manipulate. I've seen and used many frameworks in my career, but it's impossible to remove your bias while completing them. They simply become a tool to justify the decision that you really want in your gut. So cut out the middle step. Trust your gut to guide you.

If it's a new experience to trust your gut, use the approach outlined above—imagining yourself 20 years in the future looking back at the decision. Your future self always has the wisdom of 20:20 hindsight and is a voice for what you really want. If you're still having trouble, I provide another decision technique on my website to help you connect with your gut. Visit www.rustygaillard.com/decision

Mary was able to imagine herself 20 years in the future, and her future self knew immediately that pursuing the new job was the right path for her. After days of wrestling with the decision, she got clarity in a moment and made a decision.

> *Laborious thinking indicates the need for a decision.*
>
> *—Raymond Charles Barker*

What is unique about Mary's experience is that she had the courage to trust her intuitive decision. It may be unfamiliar and uncomfortable to trust your intuition. If you find yourself in this place, remember this. The kind of decision that will move you forward in life, that will enable you to reach your next level success, will not come from your head. You can only achieve the kind of success and results in life that you want if you have the courage to make a decision based on your heart and your gut. Listen to them and trust yourself.

It can also help to remember that decisions are not permanent. If you find that a decision to move forward doesn't move you in quite the right direction, you can always adjust course. It is far more effective to make progress and adjust than to stand still trying to reach the perfect decision. Progress always beats perfection.

Powerful decisions are the foundation of a meaningful life of freedom. Decide that you want it. Decide that you will have it. Your decision is the first step to breaking the code.

Discover Your InnerTech

Once you decide to break the code, the next obvious step is to rewrite it. But to rewrite the code, you first have to understand your InnerTech.

Just like the tech you use daily, like a computer or your phone, your InnerTech has three components: hardware, operating system, and apps. The hardware is you: your physical body and your past experiences. The next layer is the Operating System, which is your beliefs, thought patterns, and habits—your code. The apps are the equivalent of the life choices you make. You don't buy a phone for the hardware or the operating system. You buy it for the apps, and you install apps that reflect your priorities and your interests. Similarly, you fill your life with activities that reflect your priorities, interests, and values.

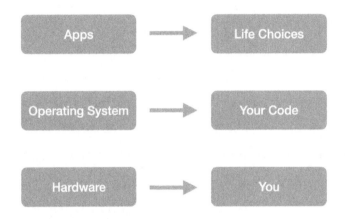

FIGURE 2: YOUR INNERTECH

All the value is in the apps. In your life, apps can be your family, career, hobbies, friends, interests, physical health, volunteering, spiritual life, and entertainment. Just as there are unlimited apps to install on your phone, there is no limit to the variety of activities and interests you can include in your life.

The operating system is what enables or limits the apps. To extend the example we've been working with so far, you can't install an "app" for a job with $300,000 salary if that is incompatible with your operating system. The app will fail. To successfully install the app, you have to rewrite the code.

The problem is that most people don't pay attention to the operating system. In the tech world, users are told never to mess with the operating system. Because everything relies on the operating system, you don't want anyone unqualified to touch it. A mistake or a bug has the potential to crash the whole system.

When it comes to your InnerTech, not only *can* you upgrade your operating system, but *you must* upgrade it to achieve your goals. Rewriting the code is what enables you to achieve a new level of success in your life.

Follow the C.O.D.E.

To upgrade your InnerTech, follow the acronym C.O.D.E.: *Confront* the limitations of what you think is possible, *Optimize* your code, *Design* your vision of next level success, and finally ***Execute*** the changes in your life.

C onfront
O ptimize
D esign
E xecute

FIGURE 3: INNERTECH UPGRADE

When you **confront** the inherent limitations of your code, you take an honest look at your life and what you believe is possible or practical for you. In reading this far, you have already confronted some truths about yourself and beliefs you hold. Confrontation is a critical first step, because it reveals what is not working for you.

In order to change what's not working, you have to **optimize** your code. This step involves identifying the elements of code (beliefs, assumptions, habits) that hold you back and updating them.

Once you have optimized your beliefs, habits, and assumptions, you can **design** a vision for your next level of success. This is equivalent to picking the apps that you want on your phone. When it comes to your InnerTech, you design the life that you want: what kind of work you do, how much free time you have, the nature of your relationships, etc. You create a vision for your life.

Your vision becomes your *why*. You have to have a compelling reason to take action or you won't take it. Simply wanting "more" or "better" isn't enough. You must design a clear vision that is meaningful to you, then move towards it.

Finally, you **execute** on your vision by taking action. Optimizing your beliefs and designing a vision isn't enough. You must act to create it in your life. Those action steps also serve another purpose—to install the new optimized code. As you take different actions and achieve different results in your life, you start to see yourself as a new person. You have rewritten the code.

Confront

The best place to begin an upgrade to your InnerTech is with a clear-eyed look at your life today. Take a moment and assess your level of satisfaction with your life. Looking across all areas of life: health, relationships, career, friendships, hobbies and interests, and free time. Are you fully satisfied in these areas of your life, or is there a desire for a deeper and more complete level of satisfaction?

This is not an exercise you'll share with anyone else. There is no one to impress, and you're not defending your life choices. Challenge yourself to look honestly at your life and ask where you would like even more fulfillment and happiness. There is nothing wrong with wanting your life to be even better than it already is. It's perfectly natural. Life is an expansive and creative process, and no matter the level of success and happiness in your life, it's normal and natural to desire an even deeper level of satisfaction and fulfillment.

You may be tempted to breeze through this exercise without really stopping to think about it. Don't do that. Put this book down for two minutes right now and reflect on your life: where would you love to feel even more satisfied? When you're done, pick up the book and keep reading.

Efficient Code

Once you have a clear picture of your life—the best points and the parts you'd like to improve—it's time to look at your code: the beliefs and habits that have created the results you have in your life.

We evolved to be as efficient as possible with the energy we consume. For many thousands of years this was critical, as food was not as plentiful as it is today. As a result, our brain is highly effective at automating routine tasks so they require less energy. Think about the first time you drove a car. You had to concentrate on dozens of variables at the same time: how hard to press on the brake or gas pedal, where to put your hands on the steering wheel, whether you raise or lower the lever to active your left turn signal, the speed limit, how to use the mirrors effectively. If you're like I was, it was overwhelming. Through repetition driving became easier and easier. Most experienced drivers can have a conversation, search for their favorite radio station, and even send a text message (I don't advise that!) while driving. The driving has become automatic. Your brain has optimized for it, and you no longer have to think about it.

You will have noticed this if you take the same roads to work every day. You get in the car and you drive, without thinking of where you're going or how to get there. Your automatic brain just takes over. I'm sure you can relate to the experience I've had many times, where I find myself on the way to work when I intended to go to the store or a friend's house. I am thinking about something else and my autopilot takes over, taking me along the well-traveled route to work. All without even realizing it.

Driving is a great example of how your brain takes in information about the environment, processes it, and responds automatically. It's something we can all relate to. But that's not the only place it happens. That same process happens throughout your life. Whether you're at work, watching TV, playing a game with family, or at the store—your brain is constantly monitoring the environment and responding to it automatically. This automatic response is highly efficient.

If something in your environment catches your attention—an email from your boss, a "look" from your spouse—your attention is drawn there and your conscious brain kicks in. Absent that, you will mostly be on autopilot. Stop and consider that. How much of your life do you operate on autopilot?

If you're like most people, 95% of your life is on autopilot. Consider these questions:

- What is the first thing you do when you wake up?
- How do you feel about your job (excitement, commitment, dread)?
- How do you greet your spouse and children when you get home after work?
- What do you do when you're stressed or bored at work?

Most people have well-established patterns in these areas of life. There may be small daily fluctuations in your habits, but the general trend is the same over long periods of time. That is the effect of being on autopilot.

Your highly efficient code drives most of your decisions and actions each day, and it was trained from your past experience. That means 95% of the time you are repeating behaviors that worked for you in the past. <u>The vast majority of your behavior is biased towards recreating your past results.</u>

If nothing changes, nothing changes. You must confront the patterns of thought and behavior that you live by and that create all results in your life. Once you confront them and see them, then you have an opportunity to change them.

Optimize

Most people operate within their code, setting incremental goals that they think they can achieve. In order to design your next level of success—a step change in clarity, confidence, and fulfillment—you have to step outside of your existing patterns and habits. You have to optimize your code.

The challenge is that your code will pull you back to your existing level of results in life. The most powerful predictor of your behavior and your results in life is your self-image. Unless you update it, you will inevitably revert to your old habits and beliefs and recreate your existing levels of success and happiness in your life. It's why most people give up on their New Year's resolutions by January. They don't see themselves as a new person. Without a change to their self-image, they can't overcome the gravitational pull of their code.

Jeff Bezos is a perfect example of someone who has updated his code repeatedly over the past decades. Most CEOs of small companies are replaced as the company grows because they don't have the skills or ability to grow with the company. What made them effective as a small-business CEO prevents them from being successful as a large-business CEO. They have to reinvent themselves to scale.

Netflix has a documentary about Amazon that shows Bezos from the days when the entire staff of Amazon fit into a small office. He was goofy, informal, and looked very much the part of a Silicon Valley startup

CEO. Now, twenty years later, he's smooth, impressive, and powerful—managing thousands of employees spread around the globe. To achieve this, Bezos updated his code and everything changed: how he spends his time, what activities he does, who he talks to, how he dresses. Most importantly, he changed how he sees himself.

Your code is the heart of your InnerTech. On your phone, the operating system is not something you think about, but it determines what apps can and can't run on your phone. The same is true with your InnerTech. When you update your code, you can install apps (jobs, relationships, income, vacations) you could not achieve before.

Bezos transformed Amazon from a startup to the world's largest bookstore, to the world's largest store, to the world's largest marketplace, and to one of the world's largest cloud computing providers. This was a process of incremental upgrades—both to the company, and to himself.

It can be easy to assume that Bezos's success stems entirely from his wealth and business position, but consider his way of thinking. With each new business idea he pursues, Bezos *believes* he can accomplish it. He thinks big—beyond what is reasonable or practical—yet he embraces the new direction not just as possible, but as probable. He optimizes his code to be aligned with the next level of success.

Update Your Beliefs

Like Bezos, you can optimize your code by changing your thought patterns. If you don't, you will keep the same patterns and habits, and you will recreate the same results indefinitely. But if you deliberately think different thoughts, you can change your automatic response to the world around you.

Consider this simple example[ii]:

> Anne goes to the bank.

Can you picture Anne on the way to the bank, perhaps to deposit or withdraw some money from her account? What if you knew that Anne was an avid kayaker who frequently went down challenging rivers, and that she took a break by paddling over to the riverbank to rest. Does that background shift your understanding of the sentence above?

> *You are not aware of the automatic assumptions you make.*

You interpret the world around you based on the most frequent past experiences you've had. Most people live in cities, not near rivers, so they interpret "bank" as a financial institution. <u>Notice that you aren't even consciously aware of making that interpretation.</u> You didn't deliberately consider the multiple interpretations of the word "bank" and choose one. Your brain did it automatically based on your past experiences. That is your code at work.

Consider the implications of that automatic processing your brain does. Your brain automatically filters out possibilities and different interpretations of situations based on your past experience. Just like you missed a possible interpretation of the sentence about Anne, you miss out on hundreds of possible interpretations about the world every day. It's hard to overestimate the impact your code has in your daily life.

You can have a short-term change in your code by changing the context. When you understand that Anne frequently kayaks on the river, you may now realize that bank can refer to the side of the river. If you repeat that thought frequently enough, you will rewire your brain with a new (or expanded) understanding of the word "bank".

That is a simple example of reprogramming your automatic response to interpret the world around you differently. You can apply that same approach to optimize your beliefs.

Look at the following statements and notice whether you agree these are logical, common sense statements.

- You can't get paid to do work you love. Work is separate from hobbies.
- Your family & friends' opinion about your job is important
- Work is hard. It requires lots of hours, sacrifice, and challenge
- You have to put on your game face when you go to work
- You have to prioritize stability until your children are through college
- You can only get a job if you have relevant experience
- Your past salary is a good representation of how much you can earn

If some part of you agrees with these statements, you have an opportunity to upgrade your beliefs.

You may have the *opportunity* to upgrade your beliefs, but you don't *have to* change them. You can remain adamant in your belief that these statements are true, and your experience in life will almost certainly reinforce that belief. But if you want to experience a different level of results in your life, you must start by changing your beliefs. The result never comes first. The belief comes first.

Open a corner of your mind to the possibility that the statements above are not true—that you can surpass these limiting beliefs and create a rich and abundant life. Should you choose to do that, be deliberate about changing your thinking. Make a clear decision to unlearn these beliefs and learn new ones in their place. You can come up with your own statements about what is possible, but if you want a head start, you can use these:

- I can get paid to do work that is meaningful, rewarding, and fun
- My family & friends will respect me for following my heart & doing work I love
- Work can feel easy, where I enjoy the time and energy I put into it
- I can be my full self at work and enjoy a seamless transition from work to home
- I am resourceful and will be able to handle everything that comes my way
- There are unlimited ways to reach my goal
- Anything is possible, whether I've experienced it in the past or not

This is not a one-time exercise. You will have to practice these statements until they start to become part of your belief system. Once they do, the door opens to a whole new possibility for you.

It's the repetition of affirmations that leads to belief. And once that belief becomes a deep conviction, things begin to happen.

—*Muhammad Ali*

To optimize your beliefs, start by listing beliefs that you hold about how the world works, and what is possible for you. You can borrow from the list above if they feel true to you. Next, write updated empowering beliefs with which you can replace the existing beliefs. Then take those new, empowering beliefs and read them daily. Post them on your bathroom mirror, on your desk, or somewhere where you'll see them regularly. Practice these new beliefs until you begin to learn them, until they become engrained. This is how you update your code.

You will never be able to consciously process the world around you. It's simply too much information for our brain to handle. But you can change your automatic processing to work to your advantage. You do this by optimizing your code. Change your beliefs by choosing and repeating deliberately empowering statements.

Design

The biggest challenge successful people face is defining a vision for their next level success that they feel confident about. This isn't surprising. Studies show that only between 2% and 7% of people have a clear picture of what they really want in life.

Early in my career, the most common career advice I heard was to follow your passion. If you follow your passion, the argument went, you will love your work, be inherently good at it, and earn financial success. It sounded great! I wanted to have work I loved, was good at, and was paid well for. The problem for me was that I didn't know what I was passionate about.

Without a clear passion, the idea of following my passion was more a curse than helpful advice. Every time I heard it, I felt like a loser because I didn't even know my own passion. It sent me down a negative spiral until I finally gave up. Forget the passion—I'm just going for a job.

Even as I took a major turn in my career, leaving Apple to start my own coaching business, I wouldn't have described it as a passion. I was excited about it, energized and motivated, but I didn't feel passionate about it. Over the following months, though, my passion for the work started to build. I loved meeting new people. I was inspired by the huge success my clients realized during our work together. I was thrilled to find I could make a living doing this work. I saw an increasing possibility for reaching and helping people in the world. In short, my energy built as I went along. And as my energy built, I developed a passion for my work.

> *You don't discover your passion, you build it.*

This led me to an important realization. You don't *discover* your passion, you *build* it. As you invest yourself more deeply into something that is meaningful to you, your passion builds over time. At some point you realize that you're doing work that you're passionate about.

The secret here is not to search for your passion, but to move in the direction of something that is meaningful to you and that is far enough outside your current pattern of success that it requires you to upgrade your beliefs in order to achieve it.

In the early stages of designing the original iPhone, the focus was only on functionality. The team did not limit the design based on what they thought was possible. They designed what they wanted and then built the technology to support it. The design drove the technology. The same is true for your InnerTech.

The design of your vision, of a life that excites you, must be aspirational. If you can achieve it with your existing InnerTech, it's not big enough. It's not enough of a stretch to go from $100,000/year to $120,000/year. Most people would argue a 20% increase in salary is pretty good, but that is not the kind of change that requires a real upgrade. Just like Apple didn't build a better version of the Blackberry, you are not here to create an incremental increase in your happiness, fulfillment, and engagement in life. You are here for a step change.

A step change in your results requires an ambitious vision that will pull you outside of your comfort zone. Even *designing* that vision requires you to step outside of your current belief system. You won't envision a greater level of success if you're constrained by your existing beliefs and assumptions about the world. Just as I never even considered being a coach because my code prevented me from seeing it as an option, you won't see possibilities in your life unless you step outside the constraints of what you think is possible. Here are three steps you can take to help you step into the zone of possibility.

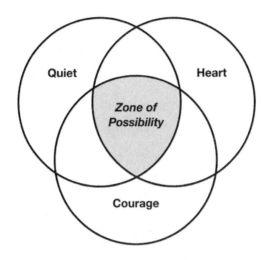

FIGURE 4: ZONE OF POSSIBILITY

1. Quiet. You will only discover what truly matters to you if you find some quiet. We live in a busy world, and we spend so much time responding to life that we don't listen very carefully to our internal ideas and inspirations. If you want to find what matters to you in life, you will need some quiet time to listen to your creative voice.

There are many ways to find quiet in your life. Meditation is a proven technique not only for quieting the mind, but it also has other mental and emotional benefits. It's not the only approach, though. You can also find an activity that you enjoy and that doesn't require much mental processing. For me that's going on a slow walk outside. The combination of movement, nature, and being away from stimulus is the quiet I need to tune in and listen to the ideas that bubble up. I often walk for exercise, but this can't be an exercise walk or my mind becomes focused on exertion and stamina. I have to slow down and give myself the mental space to listen to the ideas that arise. If you try this, leave your phone at home.

Whether you meditate, walk, or find some other activity, the key is to break out of your normal routine and intentionally seek an environment where you can relax and be creative. I've found quiet in my Sunday spiritual community, and I've had clients find it while traveling to new cities, even doing the dishes. Pay attention to what works best for you, and schedule quiet time for yourself.

2. Heart. Designing a vision for next level success is not a mental activity. It's a heart activity. Stop thinking so hard, trying to "figure out" what you would like in your life. Your mind is rational and logical, your heart is passionate and loving, and your body is strong and intuitive. If you're trying to <u>reason</u> your way to your vision of success, you're going down the wrong path.

If you're not familiar with tuning into your heart and listening to where it guides you, use your imagination to explore different ideas. Perhaps you're the kind of person who says you're not very imaginative—I've met plenty of them. But I'm sure you're quite imaginative when your loved one is late meeting you somewhere and you are unable to reach them. Everyone can imagine the worst. This is an exercise of imagining the best.

As you imagine different scenarios, make a conscious choice to keep turning up the intensity—make your vision better and better. Most people limit their imagination to a 7 or 8 on a scale of 1 to 10. Decide to turn it up to 10, even 11 (hats off to Spinal Tap). Stretch yourself to imagine a picture of your life that is so good it's beyond what you think is even possible.

I had to stretch into the impossible when I considered becoming a coach. My first thought was, "That's ridiculous! You could never be a coach." But I stretched myself. I broke the code in that moment. You have to be willing to step outside the limits of what you think is possible for yourself. Step out and ask yourself, "Would I really like that?"

As you do this, the only arbiter of success is your heart. When you imagine yourself in that possible life, does it make your heart beat faster? Does it give you that tingling feeling of being fully alive? That is your gauge. Your rational brain will have all sorts of reasons why it isn't possible, so a powerful vision will feel equally exhilarating and frightening. The feeling of exhilaration comes from your heart. Trust it. If your vision makes you feel alive, vibrant, energized, joyful, grateful, then you're on target.

3. Courage. Once you find that place of quiet and let your heart guide you, you will need courage. Your heart often leads you in a direction that you haven't been before, or that is off limits according to your code. It takes courage to imagine a different path for yourself, even for a few minutes.

As an A-player, you may be tempted to focus on <u>how</u> to achieve your vision. That is sure to limit your creativity. At this stage, when you are designing your next level of success, don't focus on <u>how</u>. Focus only on <u>what</u>.

As you're designing your life, you have an infinite assortment of apps to choose from. Any kind of work, any kind of relationship, living anywhere in the world, any income level. These are all available to you. Just as you can find an app for your phone to do anything you want, the same is true as you design your life. You can create any outcome you want.

105

If you find yourself doubting whether you can achieve it, whether it's possible for you, or how it might come to pass, screw up your courage and put those thoughts on pause. You must be willing to pause the old way of thinking long enough to create a design for a life that excites you. Return your thoughts to imagining how great it would be if it all worked out.

It may sound strange to you that it takes courage just to imagine a new level of success, but it's true. It can feel like a betrayal of the beliefs, habits, and behaviors that have helped you reach your current level of success. You may even think to yourself, "Who am I to think I could have an even better life?" This is a normal part of the process, and there is a simple way to handle it. Push pause.

Push pause on the internal voice that wants you to stay within the bounds of your current life. You only have to pause for a few minutes, but you won't find a design that really excites you if you don't. With your doubts and fears on pause, take a pen and paper and write or sketch the design for your next level of success. Include all aspects of life: your health, work, hobbies, community, family, intimate relationships. Most importantly, write in present tense, as if the design has already materialized in your life.

Trust yourself to know what new level of results you would love in your life. You have everything you need to pick the apps—to design the life—that you would love. The only thing that is required is some quiet, heart, courage and a clear decision to do it.

Execute

You optimize your code by changing your beliefs, but you install those beliefs by taking action. There's a saying in Alcoholics Anonymous: "You can't think your way into right action. You act your way into right thinking." It's through action that you install new beliefs into your code. You teach yourself that a new way of thinking is real.

When you are learning a new belief through repetition and focus, what actions can you take to help you install that belief? The simple answer is anything that reinforces that new way of thinking. If you don't believe you can get paid to do work you love, take some action towards finding and getting work you love. Think about what you might enjoy getting paid to do. Talk to a friend about it. Do some research about the job possibilities. The key here is that execution does not mean taking the "giant leap" from where you are to work you'd love. You don't have to quit your job and set off on the new path all at once. You take small steps forward. In doing so, you're demonstrating to yourself that you believe you can get paid to do work you love.

If you're skeptical about how this process works, I have seen it dozens of times personally and with my clients. I didn't quit my job on the first day I thought about being a coach. I started by talking about it, then research, then some simple math to confirm I could earn enough to support myself, then I found a place to get trained and certified as a coach. I completed the training, attended an in-person event, and met other coaches. There were scores of small steps along the way before I finally left my job at Apple. Each one of those reinforced my belief that I *can* get paid to do work I love. You can too, and you'll believe it even more deeply when you start taking action that is consistent with that belief.

When you take action towards the life you have designed, you are installing changes at two levels of your InnerTech simultaneously. You are upgrading your operating system and you are installing new apps. As you take action you are proving to yourself that the new beliefs you are learning are not just theoretical; they drive your behaviors. Remember the belief cycle. Your beliefs, thoughts, and actions all reinforce each other. By changing your beliefs, thoughts, and actions simultaneously you are engaging a powerful upgrade mechanism.

Taking action has the additional benefit of installing new apps in your life. Again, the apps in your life are the features and benefits that you really want: the rewarding job, higher salary, deep and meaningful relationships, engaging hobbies, a rich community of friends. As you take action towards these goals in your life, you are installing them into your life not as a vision or a dream but as a reality.

Execution can be easier said than done, so here are three simple tools you can use to help you take more action.

1. Seek Failure. Everyone who steps out of their familiar life pattern to move towards a new level of success will experience fear. The most common fear is the fear of failure.

- If I try and fail, I might lose the good life I have.
- If I take this chance, I might jeopardize the stability of my family.
- What will my friends think of me if I fail?

Are those thoughts familiar to you? They certainly are to me. I had all of them as I left my 25-year career to become a coach. The question is what you do in response to those fears.

Most people have been trained to think of fears as a red light—a reason to stop or remain stopped. There's biological history here. Fear is a mechanism to keep you alive from the days when we were prey to lions and bears. If you feel fear because your life is in danger, you want to listen to that fear!

The fears we're talking about here are not the same. They are not life threatening, and yet most people still treat them as a red light. The truth is they are a green light—indicating that you are going in the right direction. Your vision for next level success is, by definition, outside of your existing life experience—and anything outside of your existing life experience will generate fear.

We are biologically wired to have trepidation about a new experience, risk, or vulnerability. All of those are

111

part of the journey to step into your next level of success, so if you're experiencing fear, it means you're on the right track.

You can take this to the next level by evolving the typical Silicon Valley expression of "fail fast". Everyone agrees that failure is the quickest path to success. That's fine for an organization, but it doesn't feel so good on a personal level. You can modify that concept slightly: to *seek* failure. Seeking failure becomes a deliberate act, to push your boundaries, try new things, and actively search for the limits of what you can do. Somehow falling down doesn't seem so bad when you're intentionally pushing yourself to find your capabilities.

One final piece of information here might be useful. Psychologist Carol Dweck from Stanford described two fundamental mindsets: fixed and growth. The fixed mindset means that you believe your intelligence and capabilities are fixed: you're either good at something or you're not. In that mindset, failure means you're not good. The growth mindset means that you believe intelligence and talent can be developed over time. In that mindset, failure is simply part of the learning process.

As someone who lived many years in the fixed mindset, I avoided things where I might fail because I believed the failure reflected my capability and intelligence. My capability was a large part of my identity, and I didn't want to be seen as incapable or a failure. I've been able to shift that mindset over time (another InnerTech upgrade), and I now have a more balanced view of failure. If you relate to this, the intellectual awareness of the merits of a growth mindset can be a good cornerstone on which you build a growth mindset and an openness to failure.

2. Change your routine. You now understand that 95% of your life is lived on autopilot. You'll never achieve your next level success when you're operating from code that was designed to keep you stable at your current level of results. If you're going to achieve a new level of success you have to do something different.

> *To have something you've never had, you must be willing to do something you've never done.*

Start by changing some of your habits. If you normally check your phone as soon as you get out of bed, try putting your phone in another room and do 2 minutes of stretching when you wake up. If you normally start your workday by responding to email, try scheduling 30 minutes of planning and focused work time at the start of your day. As you break up some of the little routines that populate your day, you will engage your thinking brain more, and you'll see opportunities to do even more things differently that move you forward towards your vision.

When starting something new, we have the tendency to fall back on what has worked before. We use the same old traditional approaches. The current version of your InnerTech will not lead you to an upgrade. You must form new beliefs and habits. Doing that requires searching out and vigorously employing new ways of doing things.

As adults, doing new things is uncomfortable. We often talk about a comfort zone, but it's better described as your pattern of familiar actions, or your current code. In many cases those patterns aren't even comfortable. If you were truly comfortable and had all of the results you want in your life, you wouldn't be reading this book. Growth requires change, and change can be uncomfortable. <u>You must be willing to be uncomfortable in the interest of your growth.</u>

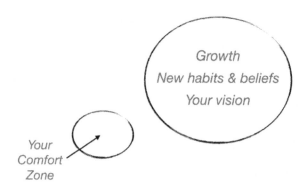

FIGURE 5: GROWTH IS OUTSIDE YOUR COMFORT ZONE

One way to build new behaviors and actions into your life is to develop a routine. My highest recommendation for a new routine is to develop a morning "power hour". This doesn't have to be a full 60-minutes, but devote time each morning to setting up your day for success.

My morning power hour has three components. I start by attending to my body. I drink a glass of warm water (everyone wakes up partially dehydrated, and warm water is gentler on the body than ice water or hot water), and I do a simple stretching routine. Next

I spend time writing in my journal. Journaling is a way to clear my mind of any thoughts, concerns, or stress that I bring into my day. After journaling, I meditate. My power hour normally takes about 60 minutes, but I flex it up or down depending on my schedule.

> *Routine is the way to concentrate and silence the voices within, in order not to listen to the voice that tells me that I will lose.*
>
> —*Rafael Nadal*

If you don't have a power hour, I suggest experimenting with one. You can start with a simple 5-minute process and extend it as you'd like. When I first started a morning routine, it was a 5-minute meditation. Start where you are and build from there.

If you've never journaled, I have a few simple recommendations for you. For journaling, start by reflecting and writing about your energy entering the day. Are you excited, tired, motivated, nervous, or afraid? Next, ask yourself what energy would be most useful for you to carry throughout the day. You are most effective when you're energized, focused, positive, engaged, and creative. Finally, set an intention for your day. An intention is not about what you are going to do, it's about how you are going to be. This can be a simple journaling process that helps you notice where you are and align yourself to the most productive state for your day.

If you've never meditated, there are dozens of apps and YouTube channels devoted to helping people develop a meditation practice. One of the ones I particularly like is "Waking Up" by Sam Harris. As he says, the point of meditation is not to be a good meditator, it's to have a good life. Enough said.

A power hour by itself will not enable you to achieve your vision for next level success, but it sets you up for success by setting your mindset for the day. With the right mindset, you will be able to take the actions that move you forward to achieve your vision.

Search out new ideas and try them on. Keep what works and discard the rest.

3. Control your calendar. Shortly after being promoted to Director of Worldwide Finance at Apple, I was overwhelmed with the number of meetings I had on my schedule. My days got away from me and I had no work time, running from meeting to meeting, most days running 5-10 minutes behind.

I observed my boss, and he was regularly calm, punctual, and often at his desk working. I couldn't figure out how he could be so on top of his schedule and I could be so frantic. So I asked him.

"I'm in meetings all the time, and I don't have any time to get work done. How do you manage to keep your calendar in check?" I asked.

His response was simple. "You own your calendar. You decide what's on it."

I wasn't very satisfied with that answer. From my perspective, I was only saying yes to the things that were important. I didn't see another path. The truth is, I was looking for something that was easier to do—some trick that would help me find more free time in my day. It took me ten years to realize he was right.

If you ever feel like you are a slave to your calendar, you have the relationship backwards. Your calendar obeys you, not the other way around. You decide what is important, and you schedule that onto your calendar.

The easiest way to do this is to proactively schedule time on your calendar for the things that are important to you. These include work commitments and projects, but also the actions that move you towards your vision. That may be exercise, family time, researching your next job opportunity, or networking with founders to start a new business. Whatever moves you toward your vision should be on your calendar.[iii]

Having a vague intention to do something without putting it on your calendar is far less successful than scheduling it. Make the commitment to yourself and put it on your calendar. And if you want to turn up the volume even more on accountability, tell someone else about your commitment. "I'm going to call Steve on Thursday at 3pm" can be the difference between picking up the phone and delaying it for another week. Used correctly, your calendar is your friend. Use it to your advantage.

Debugging

If you follow the C.O.D.E. process, you'll be well on your way to upgrading your InnerTech. As much as I'd like to say it's a one-time effort, it will require some ongoing attention. It's not unlike a regular technology product in that way. After development, new technology is rigorously tested, looking for places where it doesn't work as expected. When a bug is identified, it is corrected.

Every developer knows that bugs are part of the process. They aren't a bad thing, they are an opportunity to improve the quality and reliability of the product. With that in mind, the developer doesn't get annoyed or frustrated when a bug is found. They keep their focus on the objective. The bug is blocking them from achieving the objective, so finding it and resolving it is progress.

You will also encounter bugs as you upgrade your InnerTech. They may be obstacles, challenges, or situations that don't go the way you want them to. Don't be discouraged. These situations are an opportunity to improve the quality of your InnerTech, to strengthen your conviction and belief in your new code.

Develop the same relationship to "bugs" in your life as a developer has. See them as opportunities to improve the quality and reliability of your InnerTech. Remember that all results in your life are the product of your code, so strengthening and upgrading your InnerTech can be nothing but a positive development in your life.

As driven, goal-oriented people, it's easy for A-players to focus on obstacles and challenges, lamenting the lack of, or difficulty of progress. Don't get stuck in that place. Remember that bugs are there to strengthen your InnerTech. Remind yourself that you are only facing challenges because you are growing towards a vision of success that matters to you. Embody the confidence and satisfaction that you will feel when you are living your vision. Then bring that energy to the task at hand and keep moving forward.

Nurture your belief that you can and will achieve your goals, that the only thing standing between you and your goals is your awareness of how to achieve them. The more consistent your attention is on what you want, the more likely you are to achieve it. Your attention is like a magnifying glass on your experience and your results. Keep your focus forward, on your goal, on your potential, and on everything you learn along the way.

Simple, Not Easy

The entire process to upgrade your InnerTech is simple, but it isn't easy. It can be challenging to see the inherent beliefs that you hold. Like the fish that doesn't know it's swimming in water, you may not even recognize the beliefs that are in place holding you back.

The path of progress begins with a simple step. Decision. Decide that you will put these practices into action, and that they will work for you. If you start out with hesitation or doubt, you will get results that reflect your hesitation and doubt (remember the Belief Cycle). Start with a clear and confident decision to get the results you want from this. As a creative person in a world of infinite possibility, you can create whatever result you desire.

In the following chapters, I will share stories of clients who have broken the code. In each case, the first step is to **confront** dissatisfaction with some aspect of their life. Next they leverage that dissatisfaction as an invitation to **optimize** their InnerTech, starting with a **design** for success that is personal to them. Once they are clear on where they are going, they **execute** the plan to get there.

This is a simple upgrade process, but it is powerful. You can use it to take your life in a whole new direction, realizing a next level success that you weren't sure you could ever achieve. I've done it, and many of my clients have done it. So can you.

Chapter 5: Should I Stay or Should I Go?

Sam had built a successful career over a decade working as a professional in a large corporation. The problem was he was unhappy. Despite having changed to a new department, he still felt restless and couldn't imagine the rest of his career there. At the same time, his code was telling him to stick it out, to be grateful, and to keep going in the same direction. He had created great success in the past ten years, and he didn't want to waste it with a change in direction.

As Sam confronted this challenge and began to explore options, he felt unsure and uncertain about his direction. He had ideas, but he wasn't sure what the right choice was. There was a lot at stake, and he felt stuck.

One approach I use with clients in this situation— who are unsure about what they want—is to ask them to guess. I asked him, "If you had to guess, what would you like to be doing?" With almost no hesitation, his answer was to pursue an MPH, a master's degree in Public Health. Since he was a child, he thought now and then about a career in public health, but he had never pursued it. He pursued the more responsible corporate career instead. But the calling never went away, and he heard it once again.

You have to be in the Zone of Possibility (quiet, heart, courage) to hear a calling. A calling is the voice of your heart and listening to it takes courage. It's not easy to contemplate a change like that—to walk away from a decade of a "responsible career" and pursue something just because it makes you happy.

In Sam's case, the idea to work in public health had occurred to him multiple times during his lifetime. He had never listened to it, because it wasn't the direction he had started in. He convinced himself that he was being responsible. Like many people, he had been taught that you can't make a living doing work you love. He had followed the responsible path to a good career, and he considered his interests as hobbies, not a profession.

This dilemma left Sam with the choice: should I stay where I am, or go in a new direction. His heart told him to go in a new direction, but his code—expressed through a litany of rational and reasonable points—argued for him to stay in his successful business career. Sam had to confront this decision clearly and directly. Stay, and sacrifice happiness for stability, or go and risk losing the success he had achieved in his career so far.

When you confront your code, you will experience a strong internal resistance to any change. You must overcome it if you are going to achieve a new level of success. Leverage these tools to help you through the process.

1. Less Head, More Heart. The voice of your code arguing for the status quo can be so loud that you don't even acknowledge or dare express a new direction. As you set aside time to think about your personal vision for next level success, decide not to listen to that voice. Push pause on the "good reasons" why you would keep doing what you are doing. Give yourself space to explore ideas that you think are impractical or risky, but that are exciting and compelling. And if you have an idea that pops into your consciousness time and again, like Sam's interest in public health, listen to it.

2. **Forget Perfection**. Just as following your passion is rotten career advice, so is looking for the *one answer* to your vision for next level success. A-students always want to get the right answer, but searching for perfection is a trap. Most people have multiple ideas that they would enjoy. The key is to look for something that you would love. How do you know you'd love it? By listening to your heart. Your heart is your guide, and it will tell you based on how you feel. If you imagine yourself in that life and you feel energized, excited, and a sense of purpose and meaning, you're on the right track.

3. **Don't Figure It Out**. When you're shopping for something new, whether it's a TV or a car, what's one of the first questions you ask? "How much does it cost?" That makes sense when you consider that you were likely taught that the price tag dictates whether or not you can have that thing. Why bother evaluating whether you'd like something, let alone get excited about it, if you can't afford it anyway? For the purpose of this exercise, <u>stop thinking about whether you can have what you imagine</u>. You may think, "That's crazy. What's the point in creating a vision for something I know I can't have?" That thought is what holds you back from having it. It's the same thought that prevented Sam from considering a new direction, even though he had thought about it for years. It's your old code stopping you from even exploring something more meaningful in your life. Give yourself permission to explore ideas without figuring out how you can achieve them. We'll tackle the HOW later in the book. For now, just explore WHAT you would design into

your life if you had a magic wand and a blank sheet of paper.

> *Desire is the starting point of all achievement, not a hope, not a wish, but a keen pulsating desire which transcends everything.*
>
> —*Napoleon Hill*

Sam decided to listen to his heart and investigate the master's degree in public health. When he shared this new direction with his family, his older brother encouraged him to get a dual degree: MPH and MBA. As a successful businessman, Sam's brother knew the value of an MBA, especially considering Sam's successful business career so far. And the MBA was a good insurance policy in the event Sam changed his mind. It made perfect sense.

Sam was torn. He respected his older brother, and the arguments all made logical sense. As a typical A-student, Sam was heavily influenced by the logical argument. In fact, it was hard to come up with an argument against the dual degree. But the MBA felt more like something he *should* do, rather than something he *wanted* to do.

When you start in a new direction you often get push back. Pressure to stay the course can come from any direction, even family. They are looking out for your best interests *based on their own code* about how to live a good and successful life. For Sam's brother, that meant an MBA.

When you are just determining your vision, be careful who you share it with. It takes courage to create a vision for your next level of success that is outside the code you have lived by so far, and it takes strength to withstand pressure from loved ones who also operate from that old code.

When I decided to become a coach, I didn't tell my dad about my decision until I was ready to face his concern and disappointment. My dad's rubric for success was to pick a good company and stay there your whole career. I was choosing a different path when I left Apple to become a coach, and I knew I would get some pushback from him. It wasn't that he didn't support me—it was the opposite. He did support me, and based on his code, I was making a mistake.

Without someone helping him stay focused on his goal, Sam may have pursued the dual degree. But he stayed on track and told his older brother the MBA wasn't for him. It takes strength to hold your new direction in the face of pushback from others, especially loved ones. But your own internal voice of fear and skepticism—the expression of your code—can be even more powerful in holding you back.

You make progress when you confront and optimize your beliefs. Sam's old paradigm told him to follow the logical and practical argument—to get the dual degree, to stay disciplined, focused, and follow the responsible path towards a successful business career. That path was logical, with the MBA as a contingency plan in case the public health direction didn't work out. It was responsible, keeping the business career alive via the MBA while exploring a new direction. It was also the path of least resistance, staying in line with others' expectations of him. Following his old code, there were multiple good reasons to keep going in business.

Sam upgraded his InnerTech by listening to his heart, moving forward with courage, and embracing his innate creativity. His heart had spoken to him for his whole life about his interest in public health, but he had not listened. You can ignore your heart's calling and "be responsible", but that is not the path of a fulfilling and rich life. It takes courage to listen to your heart, as Sam did, but that courage leads you to a more purposeful life.

Courage is required because any new path is less certain than the path you've been on. How did Sam find the courage to move forward on a less certain path? By embracing his creativity. Creativity is the basis for confidence, knowing that if a new challenging situation arose, he could handle it. If he found that the path he followed was not as fulfilling as he expected it to be, he could change course. Each day he woke up was a new beginning, an opportunity to create the path and the life that he wanted to pursue.

These new beliefs were powerful, and they enabled Sam to follow his heart rather than the "logical" career path, believe he could handle it if things didn't go his way, and trust in himself rather than following the path of his loved ones.

With a clear plan in his mind, Sam moved forward with consistent incremental action. The first steps he took were small ones—networking with others in public health, researching schools. Then he got more focused, narrowing a list of schools, thinking about where he wanted to live, and ultimately selecting a few schools where he would apply. With each step he took along this new path, his confidence and energy built. When it came time to take the big step, he was ready. He quit his corporate job, rented out his house, and moved across the country to start his master's program. Upgrade complete.

Chapter 6: If Not This, Then What?

Chris had that nagging feeling that something was missing. He was successful at work, had a stable job, and had reasonable hours. Life-work balance felt good, and he had plenty of time to spend with his family and pursue his outdoor hobbies. An avid snowboarder, his Seattle home was the perfect launching point for weekend trips to the mountains, and even an occasional mid-week get away. By all accounts, he had a great life.

Chris had been opportunistic during his career, and it had served him well. He followed opportunities that fit well in his lifestyle at the moment, like an easier job that allowed him to get a master's degree part-time. He tried his hand at a startup, taking a few years to launch his own business, but ended up back in the corporate world when his business didn't get the traction he hoped. Reflecting on his career, Chris felt good about what he had done. Yet he felt incomplete. He wasn't ready to finish off his working

139

years sitting idle in the same job. He knew he wanted something more from his career, but he couldn't put his finger on it.

A-students often find themselves in this place. Many of the best and brightest follow a traditional path of success, doing everything they're supposed to do, checking all the boxes. Yet at some point find they are not as fulfilled as they would like to be. They don't feel totally off track, yet something is missing. Putting their head down and continuing until retirement feels wrong.

When we first spoke, Chris thought he should be more appreciative for his success and comfortable life. He questioned if he was being ungrateful. I knew that feeling too. I had a great job at Apple—I was an expert, had a wonderful team, surrounded by the smartest and most dedicated people I had ever worked with, reasonable hours, good compensation. From an outside perspective, I was in an amazing place. There was absolutely nothing to complain about, yet something was missing. Staying in that safe zone until I retired felt like selling my soul. I knew I wanted more, but I didn't know what that meant. That's where Chris was too.

> *In the absence of clearly defined goals, we become strangely loyal to performing daily trivia until ultimately, we become enslaved by it.*
>
> —*Robert Heinlein*

When you're comfortable enough, it's easy to ignore the thorn in your side that's calling you to look for something more meaningful. You may talk yourself out of making a change because it's not that bad where you are right now. And that's true—you may actually have a great life. But you may also be called for more.

You have to confront the truth that you long for more meaning and satisfaction in life, and you have to decide that it's worth the effort to pursue it. You have to decide your life is worth it. You have to decide that you are worth it. Chris made that decision.

The decision to make a change is not always easy. Most people want to know what they will get before they decide to change. They want some confidence that they'll get what they want—more meaningful work—before they decide to invest in the change. That's not how it works. Decision always comes first. It will feel uncomfortable, risky, and you may have some doubt about whether you will reach your goal.

The uncomfortable feeling is, in truth, a sign that you're on the right track. A bold decision to make a change, even when you can't see how it will all work out, is the kind of decision that moves you forward.

The decision to move forward for Chris was challenging exactly because he did not know what was next. If he knew where he was going, it would have been much easier to start down the path. But in fact his precise challenge was that he *did not know* what was next. He had to decide to forge ahead and trust that he would find the answer along the way.

In Chris's case, his vision was to have a job that he loved. He knew some of the characteristics of a work environment he would like, but he didn't know exactly what he would be doing. His focus at this point was on what he knew. Chris knew he wanted to feel motivated and committed at work. He wanted to work with people he could learn from and enjoyed spending time with. He wanted to work with people who valued contribution and creativity without the grind of long hours. He did not know exactly what company, industry, or role he would have, but he knew enough to move forward.

In discussing his vision, several limiting beliefs surfaced that were limiting the clarity of what he wanted. This is not unusual. His code prevented him from seeing, much less considering, certain paths. To get a clear picture of your life at a whole new level of success, you have to step out of the paradigm you've been in. Just like you can't run the latest apps on an old operating system, you can't envision a new level of success without optimizing your beliefs. There were three updates that enabled Chris to sharpen his clarity and move into action.

1. Listen to your gut. Your gut will help you decide what you really want. A-students overuse their intellect, trying to rationalize their way to an answer about what they want in life. You will never think your way to your vision, any more than you can rationalize what you want for dinner from a menu. You simply can't get there by analyzing calorie and nutrition facts. You listen to your gut—what you're hungry for.

You can test this with your vision by picturing a new level of success and paying attention to whether it makes you come alive. You know you're on the right path when picturing yourself in your vision makes you feel energized, excited, and vibrantly alive. For

Chris, he tuned into this feeling, and it guided him towards a clear decision on what he really wanted.

If you are trying to justify your decision as the "right" decision, or a "reasonable" one, you will never design an upgrade that is meaningful, engaging, and transformational. If your design for your next level success isn't bold enough that it scares you a little, you haven't been thinking big enough. One purpose of designing a new level of success is to *demand* an update to your code. If your vision for success doesn't do that, throw off more of your constraints and reconsider the question. What would you love in your life?

2. Sacrifice not required. Stop assuming sacrifice is required to achieve your goal. Chris assumed that in order to work in the industry he wanted, he had to move to a different city, take a pay cut, and work with less than the top-notch people he had been working with. No wonder he had a hard time creating a vision for a job he would love.

Stop assuming your vision requires a sacrifice of things that are important to you. You live in a creative and abundant world. There is no shortage of opportunity, there is only a shortage of people with the motivation and awareness to create the life they want. Tap into your inherent ability to create your life experience. You have everything you need *right now* to create your vision for next level success.

3. Look for both/and solutions. Most people think life is full of trade-offs, believing they can have *either* this *or* that. Instead of either/or, look for both/and solutions. Part of Chris's idea included launching his own company where he could pick the people he worked with, shape the culture, and have an impact on the world. Yet he didn't want the financial insecurity of leaving his steady job to branch out on his own. Rather than choose one of these two paths, we explored how he could do both: maintain the financial stability of employment while creating his own company. His relationship to his day job shifted as he started investing more of his time on what he

146

really wanted to do. He found that he could do both things—having what he wanted didn't require a trade-off.

Don't underestimate the power of changing your perspective to look for both/and solutions instead of either/or choices that require a trade-off. This applies in all manners of life: relationships, health, work, life/work balance, and hobbies. When you have a work trip but don't want to leave your family behind, what options are there? Virtual meetings, traveling with your family, taking an extra day off to make a special long-weekend with the family... the list of possibilities is endless when you stop to think about them. The key is to stop and think.

You'll notice that optimizing your beliefs and designing your vision sometimes blend together. This is because you have to get outside your default belief system to design a step change in your happiness and fulfillment. Thinking from your existing code will result in ideas that are consistent with it. You have to break the code even to design a new level of success.

If this seems difficult to you, consider first if you're willing to explore a new paradigm even for five minutes. Use those five minutes to consciously and deliberately push pause on the limitations in your mind. They won't go away but it's easier to pause the constraints, knowing that you'll allow yourself to think about them five minutes later, than it is to stop them entirely.

Remember when Chris started this process, he started only with a decision. He decided that he wanted career clarity and he began the work to create that, even though he didn't know at the time what that meant. You can do the same. Even if you don't know what your next level of success looks like, you can decide that you will achieve it, living with the gratitude, joy, and ease that comes with it.

As you confront the limitations in your life, optimize your beliefs, and design a new level of success, you

148

will be well on your way to having a whole new experience of fulfillment and joy in life. But nothing happens without execution. Chris took action by investing more of his time on his own business, building a prototype that he could share with others. In doing so he confronted another limiting belief, his hesitancy to share his work with others. He overcame that belief, sharing his prototype with others to get feedback, and installed another update to his code.

At the time of writing, Chris is still in process. His vision for success continues to evolve: perhaps building and selling a company rather than running it. He is getting more insight as he progresses, bringing increasing clarity and refinement to what makes him come alive. But that clarity only comes as he takes action, installing updates to his InnerTech by acting, reflecting, and learning.

If you find yourself in a place like Chris, knowing you want a change but still uncertain about what that may be, follow the process Chris took. Build a design—pick the apps—based on what you know right now. You don't have to have the "perfect" design for your life. You only need something that lights you up enough to move forward. Finding that design will require stepping outside your paradigm and expanding the possibilities. Refining it will require you to get into action.

Progress isn't always linear, as you can see. Sometimes as you move toward your goals, you get more clarity on what you really want. If you change your vision for success, that's normal. Trust yourself. You have the ability to create anything. The more you practice listening to and following your heart, the more thrilled and fulfilled you'll be with your life.

Chapter 7: Am I Living Someone Else's Life?

After 10 years in a corporate career, Bill was sure he was on the wrong track. He had spent three years in an international assignment where the thrill of living in a different country masked an underlying unrest about his career. When he moved back to the US it all became clear. He didn't like what he was doing, and he couldn't see another move that was any better. He was stuck in a career that was no longer serving him.

As he reflected on his career, Bill confronted the reality that he had started this career because it was what his family and the people around him wanted for him. He had jobs and opportunities that many people would envy, but they weren't ones that he deliberately chose. He had followed the path that was laid out in front of him, but it wasn't his path.

Bill was smart and driven, so he was able to be successful. He knew he could put his head down and

151

keep working hard, and time would slip by. But his heart wasn't in it, and he was no longer willing to waste his life following someone else's path.

He knew he needed to make a deliberate change, but he didn't know what to do. He didn't want to follow his normal routine and hope that an interesting opportunity would fall in his lap. That's not how luck works. If you're just waiting for good luck to come your way, waiting for something to appear that you might be interested in, you have a much lower chance of getting what you want. It's like sitting in your house, hungry for pizza, and waiting for someone to knock on your door with a pizza. That would be quite good luck, but it's very unlikely to happen.

If you continue to wish for something but not get it, you may start to think you're unlucky. Maybe you've never had a truly fulfilling and engaging job, or the perfect boss who respects you and gives you the opportunity to shine. If that pattern continues, you may consider yourself unlucky.

I don't believe in luck. Of course there are random events and circumstances in this world, but luck is when random circumstances align with your interests, and that happens when you put yourself in a place to see them.

If you think you're "unlucky", it is simply a sign that you're ready for an upgrade. You can spend all your time and energy lamenting your bad luck and feeling sorry for yourself, or you can get started figuring out what there is to learn and how to move forward.

There is always something to be gained, from every experience. When my wife told me she wanted to get divorced, I was devastated. I had put all of my energy and attention into making the relationship work, but I failed. It was the first significant, undeniable failure in my life, and it hurt. I couldn't imagine anything good coming from that experience. I was totally overrun with the pain and drama.

With the benefit of 7 years of perspective, I know my divorce was an inflection point in my life. I am happier, more humble, and a better person because I got divorced. It was a painful process, but I would never trade the learnings that I gained from that experience. It made me who I am. So was I lucky or unlucky to get divorced?

Once you're invested so much time and energy in your current path, the cost of switching seems too high. Without a clear path forward, you can easily lose touch with your vitality, energy, and excitement for your work, and ultimately for life. You feel lost—having done everything you thought was right, but finding yourself unhappy and unlucky where you are, without a path ahead.

Finding a new path forward always starts with a decision. For Bill, the first decision was to get help. He felt stuck, didn't know what to do, and the accountability of a coach helped him. Whether you work with a coach or not, decide to build a system of accountability. Don't let this to be a "New Year's Resolution" kind of decision, which you quickly give up after a few weeks. Make a committed decision where you will follow through. Having an accountability system, or an accountability partner, is critical.

Making a decision to create a system of accountability was the first step, but Bill didn't know what came next. He knew it was time to change but not where to go. Having followed someone else's path, or no real path at all, he was not familiar with charting his own path forward. He felt stuck knowing what would really turn up the volume on his passion and engagement with work.

The breakthrough moment for Bill came when we were talking by phone. It was a sunny day, and he was walking through a small park near the office. I asked him how he would feel if he had a job he loved. That was a starting point, to connect with the positive feelings of a job he felt good about. He didn't know what the work was, but he could imagine having work he loved. Once he felt that, I asked him to focus on environments, industries, and roles that created that feeling in him. It wasn't long until he became serious about exploring a master's degree in psychology to become a therapist.

Notice that Bill had to navigate the design process in reverse. Rather than think about a specific career and imagine how he felt doing it, he had to first imagine feeling energized and excited by his work *even though he didn't know what it was*. Once he connected with that optimal feeling, he was more creative and could tap into ideas about work that would align with that good feeling. There are important lessons in his experience.

1. A Positive Mood is a Creative Mood. It may not be surprising to you, but you are most creative and resourceful when you are in a positive mood. If you are unhappy, depressed, pessimistic, and confused about your current position (whether that's work, relationship, health, or some other aspect of your life), your brain will not function the same way as when you're happy, engaged, excited, and optimistic.

You can optimize your creativity by cultivating a positive attitude, which will help you design a whole next level of happiness and success for your life. If that doesn't come naturally to you, go back through your past and recollect a time in your life when you were happy, proud, successful, and feeling good about life. Go back to that time, see yourself there, and _feel_ what it was like to live through that. Use your past experiences to bring a positive energy to today, so you can give your brain the positive chemicals it needs to be creative.

Cultivating positive feelings enabled Bill to be creative, but he was hesitant about the idea that came to him. Leaving his successful business career to become a therapist is breaking the code. Not only was he considering walking away from 10 years in his career, but it was a stable high-paying job, and he would have to reimburse the move expenses back to the US from his international assignment if he left within a year. It would have been easy for Bill to look for a different direction. But he didn't.

Bill's ability to contemplate a major change in direction was a major update to his code. Most people won't contemplate a change like that, but Bill embraced it. To do so required him to trust his heart, trust in his inherent ability to handle any future challenges or circumstance, and to focus his attention forward on the good things to come rather than focusing on the stability and safety he was giving up.

Not everyone decides to leave their corporate job to go in a new direction. Many of my clients are very successful remaining in their current job while taking a whole new approach to how they work— increasing their free time, effectiveness, and the satisfaction they get from work. The key is to look for and embrace the updates to your code that enable you to reach your next level of success.

2. Connect to Your Creativity. If you're like Bill, feeling called in a whole new direction, here are some simple ways to optimize your beliefs. Write these down, tape them on the mirror or someplace where you'll see them regularly, and read them out loud daily.

- The opportunities in the world are limitless
- I have only one life and I will make the most of it
- I am resourceful and can handle any situation that arises
- I am learning and growing every day
- My creative potential is greater than any challenge I face
- Each day is a new beginning with infinite potential

You can use these beliefs or write your own. The key is to change your thinking, your beliefs, and your

159

actions to connect to your internal creativity and embrace the possibilities that emanate from it.

3. Move Your Feet. Affirmations are important, but they don't work without action. The challenge is that most people look at the "big" step towards their next-level success (in Bill's case quitting his job), feel afraid, and do nothing. The reality is that there are many smaller action steps to take before you get to the one big leap.

Bill was able to talk to other therapists, investigate and apply to graduate programs, even move to a new state and buy a house where he wanted to live. He was on the path towards his next-level career, and with each step he took his updates were more deeply installed. Before "taking the leap" to quit his job, Bill was building momentum.

The secret to successfully transitioning from where you are to where you're going is to keep moving your feet; to keep taking steps forward. This approach has two main benefits. First is the progress you make

160

along the way. When you have momentum towards a goal, it's much more rewarding. The first step is always the hardest—especially when you think it's a "big" one. Taking multiple small steps forward enables you to get moving and momentum, once established, will carry you all the way to your goal.

The second benefit is that these action steps install a new belief system. As he took each small step, Bill began to see himself more and more as a therapist instead of an analyst in a large corporation. Your self-image is the strongest factor in determining your actions. As Bill took action, he identified more with his new career than his old one, making each subsequent step easier and more natural.

With your design in hand and your new optimal beliefs on the mirror, what execution step will you take? If you feel stuck or afraid, trust that there is always a step you can take. You have everything you need right now. Take the step that you can, and you will build momentum. The momentum you build with that first step can carry you all the way to your vision.

Chapter 8: Am I Working Too Hard?

Even when he started the day with a single objective, John quickly was pushed off track by the flood of urgent requests and issues coming at him. He was regularly up late working and responding to email, not getting as much sleep as he wanted, and not exercising. Despite his best efforts, he wasn't making any progress against the tide of work that overwhelmed him. Life felt like a rush, like he was always behind.

John was successful by all external measures. He had a great job at a leading company in Silicon Valley, he was paid well, he provided for his family, and he enjoyed time with his family on weekends. But work was always hanging over his head.

His friends told him this was normal. "Look around you, John. Everyone in Silicon Valley works this way." They may not have said it directly, but the underlying message was, "Don't complain. You have it good, so tough it out and stop whining about how hard you're working. That's life."

The people around you have a huge influence on your code. If you're surrounded by other A-players, you are much more likely to follow that standard code: push hard, work long hours, enjoy life when you retire. But you have a choice. John's choice was to take a different approach.

Having decided something needed to change, John challenged the assumptions he held about his career. While he had worked for large companies his whole career, he had always wanted to start a company. He liked the idea of building and running something, and he wanted to leave a tangible legacy to his children. The problem was that startups are both hugely time consuming and risky. Work was already taking up more of his life than he wanted, and he didn't see how he could launch a business without all the sacrifice.

As most people do, John believed the recipe for success required more hours and less freedom. I've held that belief myself, but it's simply another line of code. It doesn't have to govern your life, and it doesn't have to be true. What if you could have the success you wanted without your job taking over your life? In John's case, he embraced a different belief and designed his vision to run a business with reasonable work hours.

This approach breaks the conventional wisdom, and you may be tempted to write it off as naive. That is your code telling you that there is only one way to success: hard work. It's even un-American to think otherwise. The American dream is founded on the belief that if you work hard, you can achieve great success. To achieve great success without the hard work feels dishonest, like cheating.

The truth is that you get to choose how you want to live your life. You can choose: (a) work hard and never achieve your goals, (b) work hard and struggle forward over many years to reach your goals, or (c) have fortune smile on you and achieve your goals much faster and easier than you ever could imagine. Which one would you choose?

John optimized his belief system by embracing the possibility that he could achieve his goals by working less. That was a major update to his code. The question is, could he do it?

You have a habitual mental and emotional state. You may even describe yourself based on these habitual states: optimistic or pessimistic, organized or scattered, positive or negative, fun-loving or hard-working. These states are not you; they are your code, and they can be changed.

John identified as optimistic, disciplined, loyal, hard-working, a perfectionist. These are all admirable traits, but they do not define John. He is more than that, and he can achieve results that are not bound by those traits. He began to see himself as productive, proactive, effective, and relaxed.

You may confront and optimize your beliefs about yourself, but you don't update your InnerTech in a single instant. The key is to pay attention to your mental and emotional state, so you know when you are operating from your old code and when you are operating from your new optimized code.

You have decades of experience operating from your current version of code. You can't expect it to be replaced immediately. There is one exception: crisis. You've certainly heard stories about people who have a near-death experience, who survive, and come out with a wholly new view on the world. They had an intense emotional experience and it changed their code in one, quick experience. I hope you don't have that kind of crisis in your life. It may be effective at updating your code, but it comes with many other challenges.

At the other end of the spectrum from a crisis, you may experience a surprise positive event. But positive life events don't change your code. Over 90%

of lottery winners have spent or lost all their winnings within a few years of their windfall. Regardless of the size of the winning, most lottery winners are right back to their original financial condition within a few years. Why does that happen? Because they don't update their code. They think, operate, and make decisions as-if they were at their original level of wealth. That way of living is not compatible with having a lot of money. The power of the extra money is no match for the power of their InnerTech, and the money drifts away from them until they are back to their original level of wealth.

Even if you have a surprise positive event like a promotion or an expected job opportunity, you will have the same fundamental results unless you upgrade your InnerTech. While the process to upgrade is simple, you have to pay attention. There is a strong temptation to go back to your old ways of thinking and doing things. It feels safer, proven, and predictable—and it is. You know what results you will get by following that way of thinking: exactly the same results that you've had so far. But you are capable of much more, and achieving that next level of success requires upgrades. The question is whether you will maintain the upgrades long enough to keep the benefits.

The change that John made to his thinking was relatively simple: that he had enough time to invest in the things that mattered to him and that advanced him towards his vision. A general idea isn't enough, though. In order to upgrade your InnerTech, you have to live by it. And in order to execute in a new way, you have to get specific. For John, there were four specific actions: to make 5 hours/week to work on a new business, to play golf or tennis twice each week, to cruise on his boat with his family and friends at least once/month, and to get 8 hours of sleep each night.

When you take new action, you will experience resistance—both when you decide to take the action, and when you actually do it. John had the support of a coach when making a decision to change his schedule, so he overcame the hesitation and concern that came with it. The question was whether he would execute when the time came.

When you face a moment of resistance, pay attention to the part of you that wants to go back to your old habits. That is your old code, trying to remain in control of your life. To move forward in the face of that resistance, acknowledge that voice but don't listen to it. Below are three of the most common ways your old paradigm will hold you back.

1. Delay. We've all been known to procrastinate from time to time. Procrastination on the things that are most important to you, that move you forward toward your vision, can be very tempting. If you procrastinate, it doesn't mean you're weak or undisciplined. It's normal—everyone does it. It's the voice of your old code, convincing you to put off something that is outside your comfort zone and feels uncomfortable.

2. Distraction. You may also get distracted when you intend to take action towards your vision. I can't tell you the number of times I checked email when I sat down to write this book. The story in my head tells me that I may have something urgent in my email, or someone may be waiting for me to reply, and that I pride myself on being responsive, so it's a good use of my time. Of course responding to email is a good use of my time, but not when it's a distraction from my writing time. Notice when you get distracted from the action that will move you forward.

3. Dissuasion. "It's not that important." "It's not the right time to take this on." "It's not worth the risk to upset my life." Have you ever thought any of those things? That is your old code trying to talk you out of an upgrade. Look out for those thoughts. They will kill your progress before you even begin.

When you notice one of the 3 Ds at work in your life, it's an opportunity to install new habits and beliefs. Instead of seeing these as signs of weakness or failure that you're not moving forward, see them as a *good sign.* They are a sign of progress. If you weren't doing something new and different, you would not experience the 3 Ds.

John confronted all of these challenges as he took time out of his work week to focus on building a new business and his health. There were times when he scheduled time to work on his new business but took a meeting for his corporate job instead. There were times he told himself, "just a few more emails" instead of stopping to get a good night's sleep.

No one is perfect. Change happens when you notice the 3 Ds and build the muscle to stick to your original plan. In the moment when you notice them, you have created an opportunity to demonstrate to yourself that you are moving forward. It's an opportunity to install a new belief about yourself. You become the person who is willing to step around the 3 Ds and make progress towards your vision.

Every time you notice these 3 Ds active in your life and still choose to move forward, celebrate your progress and keep going. The best way to install an updated belief is through action. Keep taking action, and you'll upgrade to a new level of InnerTech.

Through continuous action, John has installed updates in his life. He has launched a nonprofit venture, sleeps well, plays golf and tennis regularly, and to his surprise found a new interest in his corporate job. Having traveled down the path of entrepreneurship, he discovered that he loves guiding and mentoring others as they develop new ideas, but he does not want to be hands-on building a new business.

As he cut time out of his work schedule, John became more focused and proactive in his corporate job. Despite working fewer hours, he was able to get more done. He focused on what really mattered, made quicker decisions, and delegated more effectively. With this new level of effectiveness, he sought and received a promotion. He enjoys his work now more than ever because he changed his beliefs and approach to work, enabling him to deliver a high level of performance while still having time for his personal interests, health, and family.

If you are wondering if you're working too hard, the answer is almost certainly yes. Nearly all A-players do. Confront your belief that hard work is always the path of progress. As John demonstrated, changing your beliefs and work habits can increase your effectiveness, happiness, and success. When you live from that new empowered place—albeit imperfectly—nothing in your environment has to change. Even in the same job, you can operate at a new level of success and freedom.

Chapter 9: Is It Time For A Change?

William was feeling stuck and desperate when we started working together. He was off track in his career and unhappy. He had moved to the outskirts of Chicago to cut down on his commute, which meant he was far away from his friends and his girlfriend. During the week he didn't have time to see them, and with his longer commute he had stopped running. As an avid runner and marathoner, he had lost a big part of his life.

William was motivated to rebuild his life, and he was moving quickly. He was flying coast to coast interviewing all over the country, but what he most wanted was a job in downtown Chicago so he could live with his girlfriend, rejoin his running team, and more easily see his friends.

When I asked William to tell me about his dream job, he already had a clear picture of it. In fact not long before, he had turned down a job with that exact company. Because it was in the cannabis industry, he wasn't sure that he wanted to work there, and out of caution he turned it down—only to regret it later. He had contacted them again, but there were no jobs open and he did not want to wait. He was ready for a move.

With all the interviews he was doing, William found several job opportunities. The best option was outside Chicago. He could live with his girlfriend downtown, but it meant a few hours of commuting each day. Not seeing any better options, he accepted the job.

A week before he was due to start, they called to push his start date back by a week. My honest reaction was concern: what if they rescinded his offer? Having graduated from business school in 2001 when the economy was in decline, I had a number of classmates who had their offers indefinitely pushed back and ultimately rescinded. That came immediately to mind when William told me his start date had been pushed back. I was concerned the same might happen to him, and knowing he had already left his other job I was worried.

William saw the extra week as a gift of free time he hadn't counted on. He woke up Monday morning that week with nothing to do. He was still interested in working at the cannabis company and it was close to where he now lived with his girlfriend, so he decided to walk down and check it out. He walked down to the office, looked up at the sign over the door, and thought about what it would be like to work there. He could walk to work. He pictured himself going in the front door and imagined the view out the windows from the office above. He imagined going to lunch in one of the nearby restaurants. He enjoyed his little day-dream, then he went home.

You may wonder why William walked over to the company office. It was as-if he was commuting, but he didn't have a job there. Why would he do something like that? The simple truth is that he wanted the job, and the idea came to him. Why not?

You may remember that I don't believe in luck, or more specifically that you create your own luck. William certainly did. The next day after walking to the cannabis company's office, they called him about a new job opening. William explained his interest and told them he had just four days until he was due to start in a new job. Fortunately the company was able to move quickly. He interviewed the next day, and by the end of the week he had accepted an offer with them.

What is your first reaction to that story? Do you think William was extremely lucky?

Stop and consider that question for a moment. It's a direct reflection of your code.

You can chalk up William's job to a stroke of good luck, or you can look for the pattern. While this is a wonderful example, I have seen dozens of "good luck" events with my clients when they step forward towards their vision for a greater life. Seeing this pattern time and again tells me that it's not just blind luck. There is something more going on.

There are multiple powerful lessons in this story about William. Here are three takeaways that you can apply directly in your own life.

1. You Conceive It Before You Achieve It. You must see a possibility before you can achieve it. Part of creating your own luck is becoming aware of the possibilities that interest you. Remember the lesson of "Anne goes to the bank". Your brain automatically makes interpretations of the world around you *without your conscious knowledge*. That means if you don't get clear about what you want, if you don't first conceive it in your mind, you will never see it when it appears in your life.

That is the exact purpose of the exercise to design your next level success—to define a vision for the career and life that you most want. The design serves two purposes. It increases your awareness of it, so you know what to look for, and you know what actions to take. The second purpose is also important—that it serves as a motivation to update your code. You have to be willing to be uncomfortable to take action, and your vision has to be meaningful enough to you that you will tolerate the discomfort.

Design a vision for a new level of success that lights you up. It will serve as motivation and help guide you along the steps to achieve it. You will never achieve a goal that you don't take the time to define. William took the time, and he was able to achieve it.

2. Focus on Possibilities, Not Problems. You may have noticed that when William's start date was pushed back, my first reaction was concern that something bad was going to happen. This was my code at work, and it's an example of how easy it is for our thinking to go to the worst case... even for a coach who practices these tools daily. The good news is that you can update your default thinking patterns.

Notice when you start focusing on the worst possible outcomes and make a deliberate choice to change your focus. This sounds easy, but it requires some discipline. You may have a well-worn pathway in your brain to worry, look for pitfalls, and anticipate the worst. Each time you notice yourself going down that path, stop yourself. If it helps, you can think of it as a pause instead of a full stop. Decide to pause the negative thoughts until the end of the day, then give yourself 15 minutes to do all of your worrying and fretting. After those 15 minutes are past, let go of the worry and focus again on how things can go right.

This is a great opportunity to use your imagination for good. Worrying and anticipating the worst are powerful uses of your imagination, but they're in the wrong direction. Exercise your positive imagination by thinking about all the ways the situation would go in your favor. Every situation has possibilities, if you choose to look for them.

3. Always Do What You Can. Looking for possibilities opens the door for them to come into your life. In William's case, that's exactly what happened. He had an unexpected week off work, and the idea came to him to walk to the cannabis company where he wanted to work. There is no way William could have anticipated that he would get a call from them, and you can't draw a strict causal relationship between his practice commute and the call the next day. But you can't deny that some opportunities arise "out of the blue", and you have to be in the right place at the right time to take advantage of them.

Always take the action that you can take, even when you can't see exactly how your action will lead to the outcome you desire. Imagine you were in William's shoes. How easy would it be to talk yourself out of walking down to the company? Can you imagine thinking to yourself, "It's a waste of time. What's the point in walking down there? I will only end up feeling worse since I don't have the job."?

Ideas may come to you that seem silly, pointless, or totally unrelated to your vision. You may be tempted to follow the logical steps. Beware! Those logical steps are the result of your old code, which tells you how the world works and how to accomplish your goals. Listen to your intuition and act based on it. You don't have to understand it, but don't argue with it—honor it.

Following your intuition, trusting yourself, honoring your non-linear thinking may be one of the most powerful ways to optimize your InnerTech. As an A-student, you rely too much on your intellect and not enough on your intuition and heart to guide you. It takes courage to follow your heart when you can't rationalize the action, but you are way smarter than you know.

> *The voice for truth speaks to every person on the planet, every single day, and that voice is as loud as our willingness to listen. —Gandhi*

Your intuition is how you access the full capacity of your brain that you normally don't tap into. You certainly have heard the statistic that most people use about 10% of their mental capacity. How do you take advantage of the other 90%? Intuition.

Intuition is the voice of your inner creativity. When you prime your thinking with your vision for next level success, your intuition will lead you where you want to go. All you have to do is practice listening to it, then having the courage to follow it.

You certainly have had the experience of an intuitive nudge to do (or not do) a certain thing. Whether that's to bring a jacket or umbrella with you when you leave the house on a beautiful sunny day, or to take a different route to work one day, nearly everyone has heard that quiet guiding voice. Your opportunity is to get even better at listening to it.

Your intuition may speak to you in a way, or at a time, that is unique to you. Some people hear their intuition while they're doing something mindless (washing dishes, raking leaves), some hear it while stimulated with something new (visiting a new city), and some hear it in dreams. Intuition shows up for different people in different ways. How does it show up for you?

Stop for a minute and think about a time when you have heard your intuition guiding you. Where were you? How did you notice your intuition? Pay attention and tune in, and you will hear your intuition even more in your life.

As an inherently creative person, you have an active intuition. If you doubt that, it just means that you aren't in tune with it. Invite your intuition into your life and give yourself more space to hear it. It's a quiet voice and will require some quiet in your life to hear it. In William's case, the idea to walk to the company never occurred to him while he was frantically interviewing. It's hard to hear your intuition when you're frantic. You have to slow down, give yourself some quiet time, and listen.

Intuition is a powerful ally during execution because it can guide you to situations and possibilities that your logical brain won't identify. Like William was inspired to walk to the office, your brain may guide you to do something that could unlock a powerful next step that you never would have found logically. It is tempting to argue with your intuition—don't. Embrace your intuition and trust it, even if you don't understand it.

Chapter 10: Now What?

Each of the last few chapters opened with a story of a smart, successful person realizing they wanted to achieve a new level of success. What is your story? Where in your life have you awakened a desire for a richer and more rewarding life?

If you don't acknowledge the desire for more fulfillment and decide to take action to address it, you will keep repeating more or less the same patterns in your life. That is the power of your code. Your beliefs and habits have been a major contributor to your success in life, but they also hold you back from reaching a new level of purpose, ease, and joy in your life. If you want to have deeper meaning and more freedom, you have to break the code.

This is not to say that there is something wrong with your life. Most of the people I work with have a great life, often with jobs that others would love to have. Life looks great from the outside, but inside they know something is missing. That seeming contradiction, having a great life yet wanting to feel even more engaged and energized, is normal and natural. It's your innate creativity seeking a fuller expression through you. Listen to that desire and trust it.

Trusting that desire for an expanded life is challenging for the best and brightest A-players because it goes against the pattern they have followed their whole life: be smart, keep your head down, work hard, sacrifice now for freedom later. That code is based on delayed gratification, but it has a bug. It leads to familiar questions after you have done everything you were "supposed to" do but aren't feeling the satisfaction you expected. Should I stay or go? If not this, then what? Is this all there is?

Having dedicated so much of your life to following the code, of course you may be reluctant to make a change. After all, this code has brought you great success in life. It's natural to hesitate before throwing out what has gotten you this far. But if you don't, you will never get to the next level of success.

Our brains are automation machines. This is great from an evolution standpoint, but not great if most of your life is run on autopilot. Many of the decisions you make, the opportunities you see and embrace, and your day-to-day habits are determined by your code. Your code is based in your beliefs, which are formed from your past experiences. The result is that your decisions today are based on the accumulated experience of your past. When you are on autopilot, you repeat the patterns and reinforce the beliefs from the past. And this is mostly invisible to you. Absent a deliberate change, you will continue to follow those patterns for the rest of your life. It's your choice. Will you live by default or by design?

Deciding to make a change comes with risk. When you veer away from the tried and true path you've followed in pursuit of something better, there is always the possibility that it doesn't go the way you want. Many A-students want to see results, have a guarantee of results, or at least have a clear path to results before they're willing to break from old patterns. It doesn't work that way. You never get results before you step forward. Your next level success begins with decision.

Once you decide to explore your next level success, follow the C.O.D.E. The first step towards a life of rich fulfillment and purpose is to **confront** the areas of life where you are less than fully satisfied. Pay attention to the places in your life where you have a desire for change. Notice where you have lost the spark, the passion, the excitement for your work and your life. Notice where there are people and circumstances in your life that feel restrictive. Perhaps you can't put your finger on it, but you know that there is more to life than just checking the boxes, bringing home a good paycheck from a stable job, and waiting for retirement.

Notice your desire for more fulfilling work, more free time, deeper and closer relationships, more fun, more meaning. Cultivate that desire, not as an idle dream, but as the first step towards realizing it in your life. All change starts with desire.

As you cultivate your desire for a richer and more fulfilling life, you are certain to bump into limiting beliefs that cast doubt on your ability to achieve the object of your desire. You must confront these beliefs and habits directly. They have contributed to your success, but they also limit you from the next level of accomplishment. When you confront them, acknowledging them but choosing not to be limited by them, you open the door to upgrading your InnerTech.

Adopting empowering beliefs about yourself and your potential are how you **optimize** your InnerTech. It starts by embracing your innate creativity and living more consistently from your creative potential. The critical point is that you do this *before* you see a new level of results in your life.

This is opposite of how most people approach life. Most people believe that once they HAVE the object of their desire, then they can DO what they want, and then they will BE happy. They believe life goes in this order: Have —> Do —> Be.

Have you ever thought that way?

I used to think that was true for money. Once I HAVE enough money saved, then I can DO what I want, like buy a new car or move to a new house, so I can BE secure and relaxed. Sound familiar?

There are two problems with that approach to life. The first is that you never get "enough" because the goal keeps moving. I will always remember my friend, a financial advisor, telling me that her clients never had quite enough, whether they had $2 million, $10 million, or $35 million. "Just a little bit more and I'll be happy," they would say.

The second problem with living this way is that it's not how the world works. You don't get what you *want* in life, you get results based on who you *are*. In other words, the world operates like this: Be —> Do —> Have. First you must BE the person in your vision, then you will DO what that person would do, and you will HAVE the results you want in your life. This is exactly what the example about salary from earlier in the book referred to. Practice seeing yourself as a person making $300,000 per year, then you will do what a $300,000/year person does and be much more likely to achieve it.

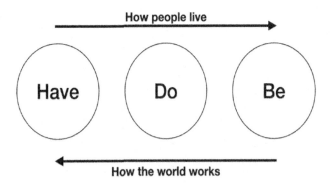

FIGURE 6: BE —> DO —> HAVE

If you think you will be more confident and secure once you have been promoted, saved $1 million, or put your kids through college, your thinking is backwards. You are assuming you will BE a certain way after you HAVE the result. It's time to optimize your code and BE the confident secure person in your vision. Once you are, you are much more likely to HAVE the results you desire in your life.

One of the most powerful ways to BE a new version of yourself is through your vision. When you **design** a vision, it serves two purposes. The first is to get clear about what new results you want in all aspects of your life: career, relationship, free time, health. When you are clear, you know what direction to go. The second and equally powerful purpose of your vision is to stretch your self-image. How you see yourself is the most powerful predictor of behavior and your actual results. Seeing yourself as the person in your vision, then thinking and acting as that person, is the most effective way to realize your vision.

Sitting in a room and picturing your next level of success will not get you to your goals, no matter how well you confront, optimize, and design. You must take action to **execute** your vision. Once again, the actions you take help you reach your goals in two ways. First by moving you towards the tangible realization of your vision, and second by confirming your self-image as the person in your vision. Through action, you show yourself that you are a different person. If you exercise regularly, you will see yourself as someone who is in shape. If you speak up regularly in meetings with your ideas, you will see yourself as a strong leader.

While I have laid out a sequential process, you will likely have observed that the steps of the C.O.D.E. process are not strictly linear. The optimize and execute steps in particular, are closely related. As you optimize your beliefs to live more and more from the energy of the person who has already achieved your vision, it becomes more and more common that you act like that person. And the actions of that person

195

will both confirm that optimized belief, and move you towards realizing your vision in your life. You must BE the person in your vision, then you will DO what that person does, and you inevitably will HAVE what they desire.

You Have Everything You Need

The steps I have outlined in this book to upgrade your InnerTech are simple, but they are not easy. You may not recognize the limiting beliefs in your InnerTech that hold you back, yet you must step outside of them to achieve next level success. If you find yourself confused, unclear, or afraid to get started, remember this: you have everything you need to create the life you would love.

You are the creator of your life. You have been given the gift of life today, and you will use this day to shape your world. You don't get a choice about that. When you go to sleep tonight, you will have created another day of life. The only question is whether you will shape it by default, based on your old code, or if you will invest the energy to shape a life by design. If there is some element of your life that you would like to change, you are 100% responsible for that change.

The changes never start outside of you—they always start with your InnerTech. Don't wait for the right time, the right opportunity, the right idea, the right amount of money. You are in exactly the right place to upgrade your life today. You may think your circumstances are what blocks you, but they don't. Don't wait for your circumstances to change. When you change, when you upgrade your InnerTech, your circumstances will change.

None of us knows how many more days we have on this planet. You don't want to look back in those final moments and regret the things you wish you had done. If you are on the fence about whether to upgrade your life, imagine yourself 20 years from now looking back at this phase of your life. From that perspective, ask yourself what actions or decisions lead to a great life. Listen to that inner wisdom and get started. You have the tools, the C.O.D.E., and the wisdom to upgrade yourself today.

There is no limit to what you can imagine, and no limit to what you can achieve. Open your mind to dream of the life that you would love and know that you can have it. If you have a hard time believing it, know that I believe it for you. I believe you can have exactly the life that you define for yourself. It all starts with a decision.

About the Author

Rusty Gaillard works at the intersection of high tech and InnerTech™, helping ambitious businesspeople achieve the next level of success by upgrading their InnerTech™.

From an engineering degree at Princeton, to his first job at GE under Jack Welch, to a Stanford MBA, to the Worldwide Director of Finance at Apple, Rusty has walked the traditional path of success. Along the way, he learned that traditional success is not the same as being successful in life. Discovering and building a successful life requires upgrades to your InnerTech™—the beliefs, thoughts, and habits that create your life experience.

Rusty has been a student of self-development and transformation for over 10 years. After many years of informal study, he was formally certified as a Life Mastery Consultant with the Brave Thinking Institute in 2018.

Rusty lives in Silicon Valley with his partner Alex and his son Teddy. He loves any activity outside, making music, dancing, and spending time with friends. A new homeowner, he happily spends weekends doing projects around the house.

Acknowledgements

This book would never have been possible without the network of support I am so fortunate to have in my life. First and foremost, my partner and strongest champion, Alex Fonseca, who always sees my ability more clearly than I do. I add my thanks to my closest friends, Dan Wedge, Dan Gieber, and Robert James who support me in being my best self.

I have worked with a lot of great people over the past year, and I appreciate their contribution to the ideas, concepts, and language I have used in the book. Notably Ellen Moore, Michael Roderick, and Tobin Slaven. I add thanks for Laura Elliott who helped jumpstart me on the writing journey. Mary Morrissey has been my mentor for the last three years, and she taught me many of the concepts I draw from in the book.

I am fortunate to have many generous people who have read drafts and provided input to the final version: Alec Kassin, Melissa Facchina, Sam Mravca,

Patty Block, David Taylor-Klaus, Tina Tran, Darcy Thompson, Merry Banks, Justin Noodleman, Nate Jovanelly, Grant Horst, Spence Hightower, Matt Jackson, Bryan Green, and Tony Coretto.

Finally, I give my thanks to my dad. He didn't get to see this book, but I could not have written it without his support and belief in me.

One Last Thing...

If you enjoyed this book or found it useful, I would be very grateful if you left a review on Amazon and shared it with others in your network who might enjoy it or benefit from reading it. Your support really does make a difference.

If you'd like to stay in touch, visit my website www.rustygaillard.com, where you can sign up for my weekly email with more inspiration, tools, and questions to help you upgrade your InnerTech™ and live on purpose.

Endnotes

i   In retrospect, become a mailman was a means of escape. I was feeling stuck in my career at that point, and I was looking for freedom. Had I become a mailman, I would have been running away from the life I had rather than running towards what I really wanted. Looking back at that time, I'm grateful that I didn't pursue it—it would have been a detour that took me away from what I really wanted: a life with more meaning and fulfillment.

ii Example from Daniel Kahneman "Thinking, Fast and Slow".

iii If you've never seen the video of Stephen Covey demonstrating the principle of "put the big rocks in first", you will enjoy it. Search on YouTube for "Stephen Covey Put First Things First".

Printed in Great Britain
by Amazon